Plays and Poems

Studies in Austrian Literature, Culture, and Thought

Translation Series

Oskar Kokoschka

Plays and Poems

Translated by Michael Mitchell
Afterword by
Karl Leydecker

ARIADNE PRESS
Riverside, California

Ariadne Press would like to express its appreciation to the
Bundeskanzleramt, Sektion Kunst, Vienna for assistance in
publishing this book.

Translated from the German
Das schriftliche Werk, Hans Christians Verlag
World Rights ©Thomas Sessler Verlag, Wien

Library of Congress Cataloging-in-Publication Data

Kokoschka, Oskar, 1886-1980
 [Selections, 1999]
  Plays and poems / Oskar Kokoschka : translated by
Michael Mitchell ; afterword by Karl Leydecker.
      p.   cm. -- (Studies in Austrian literature, culture, and
thought. Translation Series)
  Contents: Poems — Murderer, hope of women (1st
version) — Murderer, hope of women (2nd version) — Sphinx
and strawman, an oddity — Sphinx and strawman, a comedy
for mechanical dolls — Job — The burning bush — Orpheus
and Eurydice — Comenius.
    ISBN 1-57241-041-8
    1. Kokoschka, Oskar, 1888-   Translations into English.
I. Mitchell, Michael, 1941-   . II. Title. III. Series.
PT2621.0664A85 2001
813'.912--dc21   99-36779
                                                CIP

Cover:
Art Director, Designer: George McGinnis
Drawing: Oskar Kokoschka

Copyright ©2001
by Ariadne Press
270 Goins Court
Riverside, CA 92507

All rights reserved.
No part of this publication may be reproduced or transmitted
in any form or by any means without formal permission.

ISBN 1-57241-041-8

CONTENTS

Poems 1

Murderer, Hope of Women (First version) 21

Murderer, Hope of Women (Second Version) 29

Sphinx and Strawman, An Oddity 39

Sphinx and Strawman, A Comedy for Mechanical Dolls 51

Job 61

The Burning Bush 87

Orpheus and Eurydice 107

Comenius 167

Afterword 245
By Karl Leydecker

POEMS

THE DREAMING BOYS
(1907)
(Dedicated to Gustav Klimt as a token of admiration)

little red fish
little fish red
with my triple-edged knife I stab you dead
with my fingers asunder rend
to bring your mute circling to an end

little red fish
little fish red
my little knife is red
my little fingers are red
in the bowl a little fish sinks down dead

and i fell down and dreamed
destiny has many pockets
i am waiting beside a peruvian stone tree
its many-fingered leaf-arms stretch out like fearful arms and
    fingers of thin
yellow figures
stirring imperceptibly in the star-flowered bushes
    as blind men stir
without a bright
departing streak in the dark air of falling
    starflowers luring the mute animals
blood-frenzied she-beasts
slipping away
in fours and fives out of the green
breathing sea-forest
with its silent rain

above the forest waves pursue their crashing course
    through the rootless
red-flowered

2 Poems

countless air-branches
which like hair dip sucking into the seawater
where green rollers writhe their way out
and the terrible ocean of depths and
    man-eating fish
seizes the overcrowded galley
    up on the masts swing cages with little
    blue birds
pulls on the iron chains and dances with it
    out into the typhoons, where
        water columns like ghost snakes walk on the
        roaring waters
I hear the calls of the sailors
heading for the lands where birds can talk
the sails tossed this way and tossed that
cold air stirred them and twisted the canvas
the ship docks
softly and in step
at intervals audible
then at times drowned out go the processions of those
    disembarking
fawners in brown woollen clothes worm their way through
    and naked skinny girls give birds
nuts and coral necklaces in memory
    of the nights of dark caresses
and i fell and dreamed the sick night

why do you sleep
blue-clad men
under the branches of the dark walnut trees in the moonlight?

you gentle women
what is that welling up in your red coats
in your bodies the expectation of entwined limbs
    since yesterday and time immemorial?

do you feel the excited heat of the quivering
mild air
— i am the circling werewolf —

when the sound of the evening bell fades
i creep into your gardens
into your pastures
i break into your peaceable kraal

my body divested of its harness
my body enhanced with blood and paint
crawls into your bowers
swarms through your villages
crawls into your souls
swarms in your bodies

out of the most solitary silence
before your awakening my howling rends the air

i devour you
men
women
halfwaking listening children
the frenzied loving werewolf within you

and i fell down and dreamed of unstoppable changes

harro
out of the yellow
stagnant water
in which you live like stony corals

harro
you with waxy complexions and doughy masks and
    beards of red mold
a wind blows into the forgotten city

in whose locked rooms singing people
    hang as in birdcages

harro
you large fearful congregation
my weak boy's song and my innocent's prayer
    no longer guards your vices

there is dreaming inside me and my dreams are like the north
where snow-mountains hide ancient fairytales
my thoughts go through my brain and make
    me grow
as stones grow
no one knows and understands

for fearful hours i dream sobbing and quivering
    like children
who leave their beds as adults

it is not the events of childhood that go through me
    and not those of manhood
but boyishness
a hesitant wanting
unfounded feelings of shame at growth
and youthfulness
the overflowing the aloneness
i recognized myself and my body
and i fell down and dreamed love

first i was the dancer of kings
in the thousand-stepped garden I danced the wishes
    of the sexes
danced the thin spring bushes
before you li
    — maid your name tinkles like silver foil —
    stepped out of the falls of cinnabar flowers

      and yellow sulphur stars
out of the spice gardens
i knew you and awaited you
    on blue evenings on my silver blanket
out of the tangled birdforests of the north
    and from the lakes of the red fish of the south
i sensed you coming
felt the gesture of the angular twist of your young body
    and understood the dark words of your skin
    and of your childish wrists hung with glass beads
and i fled from you into the gardens
upward from step to step
to the thousandth and last of my shyness
music
music
tumbler my body
bell-rattler
cymbal-clasher

away from me bogey of my sinful restraint
bright fires are on the dwarf forests
down to earth i leap with fluttering garments
    and behind me like a single high note longing
    hangs over the gardens
and i dreamed
like a tongue-moist tree is my body

in lost springs life runs up and down
    threatening to overspill
the nights of wondrous
nameless creatures carry my love away and
    out of my tangled inwardness there is no reaching out
    to others' clutching fingers
which would be without memories
i wait once more in my hut
from the bank two otters ran over the clay

6 Poems

    of the treeless plain
a girl visits me
your thin unmarked fingers should
    cling to my knees like full-blown blooms
the green tree loves you and your red
embroidered hands on my blanket in the hut
i say out loud
the sea-grass on which you are lying loves you
and i guess i say too
a man loves you
a man lying beside you on the sea-grass in the hut
    under the green tree
and hear not
that the noiseless silence remains

like a sole man i see you
i should perhaps have gathered shells for you

i am the sole man
who knows of you
what awaits in spring
but that is not to speak of an unformed thing
when the skin does not yet know
we will have to search
as for a lost child

as for something
left hanging in the air and unspoken

and i fell down and dreamed toward morning
you are to stay in my house
i do not want to sleep

i must clutch at the air with my hands
    and call for you down the passageways
although i am ashamed

no man has ever seen you as i have
i stand beside you and see your arm bend
the kind of tale
which ceases to be
when one touches it
beyond all words and signs i see
oh how i rejoice
that you are like me
how you are like me
come no closer
but live in my house
    and i will look for the childish
    trembling of your shoulders and see
how your mouth
without seeking words
speaks for me

in my white room i was alone
but perhaps now i carried you in and something stays
and speaks to me as from heavy blooms
my room became like another country
i enter the white forests
in all white forests a reindeer's hoof rings out and throws
    up glistening snowstars
all round you it is like lacy gardens
reindeer-rider
and the reindeer is a mountain
your clothes are a snowfield
where flowers appear
the touch of your thin fingers
and the snow forests stand round you like marveling boys
the snow melts to form a lake
    and you were sitting on a little red fish
of you i had seen only your naked neck
    in your hair

a little rod grows down into the water
where the end of all being is

out of your round breast your breath goes over the blue sea
how quiet are the workings of all being
i reach into the lake and plunge into your hair

like a dreamer i am in my love of all being

and again i fell down and dreamed

too much heat overcame me in the night
as in the forests the mating snake sheds its skin
    under the hot stone and the water-deer
    rubs its antlers
    on the cinnamon bushes
when i smelled the musk of the animal
    in all the low shrubs

it is strange around me
someone should answer
everything follows its own trail
and the humming of the gnats drowns out the screams

who thinks of grinning gods' faces and questions
    the singsong of the magicians and elders
when they accompany the boatsmen
bringing women

and i was a creeping thing
when i sought the beasts and stayed with them
little boy
what were you looking for beyond the old men
when you sought out those who conjure up god

i staggered

when i recognized my flesh

and i loved all things
when i spoke to a girl

THE WHITE ANIMAL-SLAYER (1907-17)

Some time after, I saw a white bird close by my foot. When it had attracted my attention, it ran in front of me, not shy, nor appearing frightened, following the twist of the terrain toward the brightness of the full moon. For a long time I tried to keep it in view until everything disappeared apart from the light surrounding me.

Visible on the disk of the moon, true-to-life, in the attitude of waiting, was the figure of a woman. I stared at the apparition for a good while without noticing that, drawn by her, I was passing through space overcast with clouds of restless, buzzing creatures. Then everything begins to hatch out, to fly up, falls back to the ground, digs its way into the earth. I have been ill ever since that moment when the animal excitement was all around me. After a short distance, when I had reached a place which promised a view, I turned and saw that the creatures were no longer there. Then, however, I noticed something about myself (by chance, the way you observe things passing outside) namely that I had changed my face into that of a dark being with piercing eyes. There are some of that type which live buried in the solitude of the mountains.

And indeed it was only through my youth that sometimes, since then, amid my passion, I thought myself happy. What has childhood to fear, practicing in play on a wasteland! Childhood, which would so gladly abandon itself to all terrors, oh, if they would only come! Buds too, when frost and wind attack them at an unexpected season, sicken to meet the sun. I desired nothing but to die and to see things die. Everything that huddles together on the ground, beneath it, or in the air above, scaled, feathered animals, furry animals, and all that love heat.

"Son, we have to grow older. By the time my milk has dried up, we will perish." Thus, blushing, giggled the woman in the moon; she had a veil in her hand, swept into it and went behind a cloud.

"Oh sign of midnight! I was a valiant drinker, drank for ten years in a row milk from your udders. Fear nothing, now that I am about to swap your milk for your blood!" Getting her breath back with the leaping fire-mountains which bark at the moon, gurgling as far

as the receding sweep of moonlit sandy plains, my cruel love barked out:
"How I must scold your hot love! My sides are already quite bloody, as in thornbushes, from your clumsy hands!" she cried, then went and put the moon out completely.
I felt tired, would have liked to have been at home, threw a stone to chase away the white bird, and fell fast asleep out in the open. Womanly children, who want to be kissed, pass through my mind, bunches of womanly children observe me, each letting go of the others' hands like mulberries detaching themselves from the stalks, the berries which redden themselves are they.
The blood leaves their cheeks then colors them again because they are in love.

I felt as if dogs were barking and cocks crowing, without waking me from my paralysis, and then as if a rift in the clouds were flooding a house with light and drawing, as if with lines of chalk, in through the door, which was not bolted.
Sleep, the dream of the girls, the ray from the clouds are messengers from her, leading me, who, still half asleep, follows them into the house, to the bed where a girl kisses me in violent jest!
"What I am doing with you is because I was thirsty and there is no one here who asks me to drink out of his glass!"
"But how did it come to that?" I stammered.
"Aren't you just a little darling, you'd like to take a stroll in my blood! Come," she answered.
I hid my knife under pillows.
"Could you not be saved?" I answered myself, because the girl's body was dead, while the thought of her was still busily alive.
And, counting backwards, I worked out the time she took with calls for help, the time her body needed to fall down, and it was just the time of a moment previously, when I had been outside the walls around the house and could not get through, to get to the girl, as the only one who was prepared to undo the disaster. At that moment time, and all that went before, had disappeared for me.

Now I was sitting, alone and abandoned, beside the bier, and was in love with the nightmare, which ever more frequently visited my sad thoughts, extinguishing the guilt in them to and fro.
One night she eased the guilt completely, bid me be still and wait for her. Soon she returned in a white gown, her hair loose, and set wedding dishes on the table.
Jugs with warm cow's milk, loaves of bread, whose baking smell floated perceptibly round the room, and small, sweet fruits, which her fingers arranged.
As sparrows peck at grains, she went on to take a plate with fruit for herself as well.
"Has my little darling child been suffering deprivation for three years now?" she asked, served and looked at me, held the milk-jug to my lips and smiled, because each was gazing fixedly on the other, outdoing the other in tender modesty.
The charming serving wench puts a flapping redfish on a dish and comes to me beneath a rainbow:
"On land I am a shadow under the mirror of the day, at night liquid fire when you drown in your dreams. I cannot forget your kisses!"
Can there be such forgiveness on earth?
I blinked at the light. "Do you want my eternal life?"
As the tension on a rope is released, with a twang came her one word, "Come."
"Maybe you are deceiving me with a miracle that licks my cheeks, humble as a dog?" I quickly put a cloth over my eyes as she reached out for me. She dried my tears with the cloth and looked at me, hardly disconcerted, with a delightful, mocking smile.
"Maiden without shape or form, why do I weep? Is it because you feel nothing as your lover hides in the bushes. Somewhere in the house, you must have met him too? Even in my arms, your face stays pale." As if to dismiss the reproach, with the back of her hand she rubbed some red into her cheeks, but it quickly faded again. "Or is it because every girl will be able to point a mocking finger at me: Look at him, he's holding nothing in his arms, he's diving into the air, trying to unite with the one with whom he spends his nights. It cannot be a human girl?

"Why have you not made an effort, you who are versed in so many things, to bring home the boy whom grief binds to you because you left him behind, so that he is half dying with yearning, throwing himself about in the sheets, not living nor dead.
"But I fear all this is but a dream.
"If you had only left your trail behind, by that thread I would find death!"
As by a wall she seemed separated from me.
She regarded me with worried looks, and her voice suffered even more.
My melancholy was replete with desiring her.
Then she closed her eyes and I no longer recognized her.
She fled and gasped, "The most humble of women I remain, in spite of everything. Before you step into the long night I will take you on my lap."
Years had set, like the sun, many times beyond the sea.
Light as a feather, an oar pushed these years through life, and I often cast a net: hope. And if it came back: to my disappointment, without answer, without sign or letter to my flood of hope, the dead girl sent the captive waves bobbing back.
In the end I was creeping around, already completely disheveled, and cried out against senseless violence, "What a cur I am, that only in my dreams do I try to seize what is good!"
"The gifts of friendship are not to be discussed. Nothing less you have acquired than the long dream. Young man, no longer will you wake. With the sureness of a dreamwalker, you will plunge into a tumult of bliss! I no longer ask, because you love me to exhaustion. Is what is dissolving you hurting you?"
I questioned this voice, "Can I now take off the warm garments I am in?"
"Yes! Try to cross the dark bridge, young people practice death from the very start."
And I went with joy to the shore of the sea from which the moon had just risen resplendent. I dived under and felt a thin hand moving above me. It was combing my hair.

"You scoop me up out of life yourself and let me run through your fingers, you playful girl!"
"I will lay down beside you and do with you what must be done to make you the same as me."
"A high tide has come! Most lovable of girls, I am wading around, wringing my hands, how much I would like to grasp, because all the brimming floodgates are opening with a foaming torrent, an open bed pouring out, but I will come through, to you, moonwoman!"
She began to tremble, laid her pale cheeks like a lamb in my lap and took my hot fingers to her lips and embraced me and was known to me, heart to heart.
Then she emerged from the water, her arms loaded with me, laid me down on the shore and pressed her fingers into my eyes and shaped my face in the dark earth, in the dust, which in its barrenness, moves love to leave it the mortal remains. Different in essence from me, feverish with expectation, my love-ghost, my soul, no longer bound by any earthly cloak, rose over my own body.
"Moonwoman, is it permitted, now that I have lost my body, for us to stay together? And, oh! moon maid, was it the last time we come together in the world, since you arouse such endless longing?
"And that is how you came to have a child, that has been put under a spell by you, until it has forced you to its own will!"

Αλλοσ Μακαρ

Αλλοσ

How wondrously thrown out of joint I, since out of a world of mist
    a white bird called on me, Αλλοσ
Αλλοσ, to seek her, with whom I never came face to face. Because
    in that moment quickly she transformed herself into my being,
as if through
    a back door.
Suffer, ears! Strive, eyes, to see her!
I am the poor summer's night
which disappeared
and is crying from a crevasse.
Which before your human eyes
is weaving and spinning a net of golden locks.
Catches the heroes; drawn by danger.
Only gird your love-nest more mysteriously,
façades of apparent resistance a parapet round you
compelling the bird-catcher, aroused with love, to fall in your net.
Like scaled or feathered beasts, aimless,
like a hairy, naked specter, free in name alone,
you are not!
Everything that holds to the earth, bisects the lonely air,
seeks the warmth of others,
you are not, you cannot be!
In the brightness of the sun's clear rays
which, hot and strong, the world embrace,
and unbolt the womb of forms to the night-dark ones,
your net still spellbinds her who the herd's trail scorns.

Μακαρ
I come from far away,
her child the mother dropped

through foaming space.
Contentiously day and night everything cloak,
uncertainty, setting off echoes, in the breast provoke.
Awake and full of dazzlement, he comes this way.
He receives no gentle help from moon and sun,
as he climbs up, as he journeys on.
And in the misty north he took to wife a woman.
His eye went blind in the service of the fettermaker-woman.
On the heels of winter gloom,
weary of wing, longing comes.
Monsters dire they burn a fire,
both, that consists of me.
If sleep would only overcome her! Fleeing end
the nightmare of love-nooses! Hands!
If the wind should flee home
water will find its way home.
A dream I signified,
who turns the mirror for me:
liking simply calls out for itself!
Moon, lengthen one of your beams
to direct the refugee
and tell the sun to shine more softly.
Μακαρ up in the wind will sweep
Αλλοσ cling on to the deep.
Ghost-ship hanging in the air,
may mast and anchor guide you there.

Αλλοσ Μακαρ

The ribs weave round the deceptive calm.
The heart itself within assaults and presses.
From the winter sun white soil
floats back onto what is past.
Quietly over the imagined vision
the same drift grinds the dust-formed shadow-play.

A swoon comes to rest in unrest.
The heart beats like thunder, alone and distressed.
Then from below was heard
the hoarse cries of birds.
A cock and a hen are strangling a snake.
Each fears the advantage the other might take.
Each wastes its strength keeping the other at bay
and out of the raucous beaks
the snake worms its way.
Lets fall a scrap of paper, a scuffle-torn screed.
Bending low in the dust, I take it and read.
My lips smile at the deceptive calm.
"In other wise is happiness."

DEDICATION
(1914)

A man uncertain must win a battle
To dispute with the clinging rust of thought.
A bloom of mold set over his brow would
    deprive him of all pleasant outlook,
Of a span of timid light.

You see Egyptian darkness touched by a light,
Fast as you cannot rush! Will it stand firm,
The treacherous cover beneath your feet?

Only when the world wriggles free of the darkness
    pouring forth from you,
Land, dry land beneath your feet,
    will you gladly go without
    the world of your own melancholy limitation.
Enclosed in a narrow space,
    to dissolution you will pass
    through this dividing wall.

DAISY
(1920)

With lidded stare
The morning star sees
My limbs laid bare

So that from my bed I spring.
My belt ungirt.
Torn by the man I sing.

Oh such whiteness would my body please.
Red from it you have wrung.
One drop of another's clung
to the white shirt.
And where from veins, wounds, pours blood
Since it was wrapped round me as a shroud:
Rigidly following the dagger out of pain.
My friend! I have been slain:
All your caresses cannot make that undone

And it was from evening until morn.
What as lees soured your intoxication,
Out of my cup wine.
The black thought, your reprobation.
Oh let that, my love, be the hope of mine.
I am crying my fill to get well again.

MURDERER, HOPE OF WOMEN

(First version, 1907/1910)

22 Murderer, Hope of Women

CHARACTERS

THE MAN
THE WOMAN
CHORUS: men and women

*

Night sky; a tower with a large, red iron cage-door; torches the only light; black ground rising to the tower in such a way that all the characters can be seen in outline.

THE MAN
White face, blue armor, bandage covering a wound on his forehead; with him his horde of men (wild-looking, gray and red kerchiefs, white, black, and brown clothes, signs on their clothes, bare legs, long torch-staves, bells, clamor) creeping up with torches and staves outstretched, trying, wearily and sullenly, to hold the adventurer back, pulling down his horse; he advances, the ring round him dissolving as the men cry out in a slow crescendo.

MEN We were the blazing wheel around him. We were the blazing wheel around you, stormer of sealed strongholds!

Forming a chain once more, they follow him hesitantly; he leads the way, with the torch-bearer going before him.

MEN Lead us, pale one!

As they are trying to pull down the horse, women with their leader come up the steps on the left.

THE WOMAN *Red clothes, yellow hair worn loose, tall; loudly* With my breath the blond disk of the sun flickers into life, my eye gathers men's exultation, their stammering lust prowls round me like a beast.

Women break away from her, only now seeing the stranger.

FIRST MAIDEN *lasciviously* In greeting his breath has sucked itself fast onto the virgin.

FIRST MAN *in response; to the others* Our lord strikes dumb like the moon rising in the east.

SECOND MAIDEN *withdrawn, crazed* When with joy will she conceive?

The chorus breaks into groups which prowl round the stage, listening; the Man and the Woman meet in front of the cage-door.

Silence

THE WOMAN *sees him, spellbound, then to herself* Who was the stranger who saw me?

Maidens press forward

FIRST MAIDEN *recognizes him, screaming* His sister thrust a dagger to her heart because he left her a virgin!

SECOND MAIDEN Time a-singing, flowers ne'er before seen!

THE MAN *astonished; the column of the living comes to a halt* Am I real, substantial? What said the shade?

Raising his face toward her Did you look at me, did I see you?

THE WOMAN *in fear and longing* Who is the pale man? Hold him back.

FIRST MAIDEN *with a piercing scream, running back, lasciviously* You mean to let him in? He will strangle my little sister praying in the temple!

FIRST MAN *to the maidens* We saw him walk through fire unharmed.

SECOND MAN He does violence to animals, his thigh crushed whinnying mares.

THIRD MAN We had to put out the eyes of birds that ran in front of us, let red fish choke in the sand.

THE MAN *angrily, railing* Who is the woman, proudly grazing among her own like a beast?

FIRST MAN She divines what no one understood.

SECOND MAN She senses what no one heard.

THIRD MAN They say shy birds come to her and let themselves be caught.

Maidens at the same time as the men.

FIRST MAIDEN Lady, let us flee! Douse their leader's lights!

SECOND MAIDEN Lady, slip away, poor songstress.

THIRD MAIDEN He must not be our guest, breathe our air. Let him not enter, he puts me in fear.

The men press forward hesitantly, the women crowd anxiously together. The Woman goes toward the Man, crawling by fits and starts.

FIRST MAIDEN He is without desire!

FIRST MAN She is without shame!

THE WOMAN Why do you bind me, Man, with your gaze? Devouring light, you confuse my flame, consuming life comes over me, flame-tip. O take this terrible hope from me — and you will be overcome with torment —.

THE MAN *flying into a rage* Men! Burn my mark into her red flesh with hot irons!

The men carry out his order. First the Chorus with the torches struggling with her, then the Old Man with the branding-iron tears open her dress and brands her.

THE WOMAN *crying out in fearful pain* Beat them back, the cold, devouring corpses!

Leaps at him with a knife and slashes a wound in his side. The Man falls.

MEN Flee this man possessed, strike the fiend down! Woe to us in our innocence, consign the conqueror to the earth.

THE MAN *convulsions; singing with a bleeding, visible wound.* Senseless desire from horror to horror, insatiable gyration in the void. Labor without birth, sunfall, heaving space. End of those who praised me. O, your pitiless word!

MEN We know him not. Spare us! Come you singing maidens, let us unite in wedlock on the bed of his plight.

MAIDENS He puts us in fear. *To the men* You we loved, before you came.

Lie down on the ground with the men, rolling and coupling, on the right.

Three men on the wall lower down a coffin with ropes; the Man, still making slight movements, is laid in the tower, women shut the door and withdraw with the men. The Old Man gets to his feet and locks up, all is dark; soft blue light from one torch high up in the cage.

THE WOMAN *wailing, in vengeance* He cannot live, cannot die, he is completely white.

She prowls round the cage in a circle like a panther. Burning with curiosity, she creeps up to the tower, stretches a lascivious hand out toward the bars, draws a large white cross on the tower, bursts out into a scream.

Open the door, I must go to him!

Shakes the bars in despair.

MEN AND WOMEN *amused, in the shadows, jumble of voices* We've lost the key — we'll find it — have you got it? — didn't you see it? *To the Man and Woman* We are not to blame for you, we do not know you —

They go back. A cock crows; it gets lighter in the background.

THE WOMAN *putting her arm in through the bars and placing her hand in his wound, gasping with lascivious malevolence, like a viper.* Pale man! Do you flinch? Do you know fear? Are you merely sleeping? Are you awake? Do you hear me?

THE MAN *inside, breathing heavily, raises his head with a great effort, later moves one hand, then slowly stands up, singing higher and higher, becoming ecstatic.* Wind that blows, time after time, solitude, rest, and hunger confuse me. Worlds circling by, no air, evening grows long.

THE WOMAN *beginnings of fear* So much life flowing out through the crack, so much strength out through the door, pale as a corpse he is.
Creeps up the steps again, her whole body quivering, exulting once more and screaming in a high voice.

The Man has slowly stood up, leans against the bars, slowly growing.

THE WOMAN *growing weaker, in fury* Here in the cage I am taming a wild beast. Is your song baying with hunger?

THE MAN Is it I who am real, substantial, you the dead one, tangled in the net? Why are you growing paler?

A cock crows

THE WOMAN *quivering* You, a corpse, slander me?

THE MAN *powerfully* Stars and moon, devouring lights, Woman! Wounded life, dreaming or waking I saw a singing being. Breathing, a darkness takes shape. Who is feeding me?

The Woman is lying fully on him, separated by the bars, to which she clings in the air, like a monkey.

Who is suckling me with blood? I feed on your blood, I consume your dripping body.

THE WOMAN I cannot let you live, you vampire, feeding on my blood, you weaken me, woe to you, I will kill you — you shackle me — I took you captive — and you hold me — let go of me, bleeding one, your love has its arms clasped round me — as if with chains of iron — throttling me — let go — help. I lost the key that held you fast.

Lets go of the bars, writhes on the steps like a dying animal, clenching her thighs and muscles.

THE MAN *standing erect, tears open the door, touches the woman with his fingers; she rears up, rigid, all pale; recognition of death, extreme tension, which is released in a single, slowly diminishing cry; she falls down dead, falling she pulls the torch out of the hand of the leader as he stands up; the torch goes out, enveloping everything in a shower of sparks. He stands on the top step, men and women, trying to flee from him, run, screaming,* The Devil! Tie him down, run, everyone for himself — lost! *straight at him; he swats them like flies and goes off, red. A long way off a cock crows.*

MURDERER, HOPE OF WOMEN

(Second version, 1907/1916)

Dedicated by the author to his loyal friend,
Adolf Loos

Murderer, Hope of Women

CHARACTERS

THE MAN
THE WOMAN
WARRIORS
MAIDENS

The action takes place in antiquity. Night sky. Tower with a large grated iron door. Torchlight. Ground rising to the tower.

THE MAN
White face, blue armor, bandage covering a wound on his forehead, with his horde of men, wild-looking, gray and red kerchiefs, white, black, and brown clothes, signs on their clothes, bare legs, long torch-staves, bells, clamor. They creep up with torches and staves outstretched, trying, wearily and sullenly, to hold the adventurer back as he presses on, pulling down his horse. He advances. The ring round him dissolves as the men cry out in a slow crescendo.

WARRIORS We were the blazing wheel around him. We were the blazing wheel around you, stormer of sealed strongholds!
Forming a chain once more, they follow him hesitantly; he leads the way, with the torch-bearer going before him.

WARRIORS Lead us, pale one!
As they are trying to pull down his horse, maidens with their leader come down the steps on the right, which lead out of the castle wall.

THE WOMAN *Red clothes, yellow hair worn loose, tall; loudly*
With my breath the blond disk of the sun flickers into life. My eye gathers men's exultation. Their stammering lust prowls round me like a beast.

MAIDENS *break away from her, only now seeing the stranger.*

FIRST MAIDEN *full of curiosity* Our lady! His breath clings to her.

FIRST WARRIOR *in response; to the others* Our lord comes like the day rising in the East.

SECOND MAIDEN *naïvely* When with joy will she embrace?!

THE WOMAN *looking the Man firmly in the face* Who is the stranger who looked on me?

FIRST MAIDEN *pointing at him, screams* Driven-out boy-child of the mother of sorrows, snakes wreathing his brow, made his escape. Do you recognize him?

SECOND MAIDEN *smiling* The abyss quakes. Will it drive away our dear guest?

THE MAN *astonished, the column halts* What said the shade? *Raising his face; to the Woman* Did you look at me, did I see you?

THE WOMAN *in fear and longing* Who is the pale man? Hold him back.

FIRST MAIDEN *with a piercing scream, running back* You mean to let him in? One who senses we are unprotected? The stronghold stands open!

FIRST WARRIOR All things are subject to him, those that share air and water; those that wear skin and feathers, or scales; ghosts hairy and naked alike.

SECOND MAIDEN Furrowed, our Golden Curls is crying and laughing there. Huntsman, come and catch us . . .
Laughter

FIRST WARRIOR *to the Man* Embrace her! The whinnying is driving the mare crazy! Give the beast a taste of your thighs!

FIRST MAIDEN *artfully* Our Lady is in her cocoon, has not yet taken on form.

SECOND MAIDEN *boastfully* Our Lady rises and sets, But never comes to earth.

THIRD MAIDEN Our Lady is naked and smooth, Nor does she ever close her eyes.

THIRD WARRIOR *to the Third Maiden, scornfully* Little fish gets caught on hook. Fisherman will hook himself nice little she-fish.

SECOND WARRIOR *to the Second Maiden; he has understood* Flying curls! Her face set free . . . The spider has come out of its web.

THE MAN *has raised the Woman's veil; angrily* Who is she?

FIRST WARRIOR *urging him on* Wary she seems, dare you bear her off. Fears do but ensnare. Beware what you snare.

FIRST MAIDEN *fearfully* Lady, let us flee! Douse their leader's torches!

SECOND MAIDEN *obstinately* Mistress, here let me await daybreak . . . Do not bid me sleep, This restlessness in my limbs!

THIRD MAIDEN *pleading* He must not be our guest, breathe our air. Do not let him spend the night here. He will frighten away our sleep!

FIRST MAIDEN He has no luck!

FIRST WARRIOR She has no shame!

THE WOMAN Why do you bind me, Man, with your gaze? Devouring light, you confuse my flame! Consuming life comes over me. O take this terrible hope from me —

THE MAN *flying into a rage* Men! Burn my mark into her raw flesh with red-hot iron!
Warriors carry out his order. First the troop with the torches struggling with her, then the Old Man with the branding-iron tears open her dress and brands her.

THE WOMAN *crying out in fearful pain* Beat them back, the evil scourge!

Leaps at the Man with a knife and slashes a wound in his side. The Man falls.

WARRIORS Flee this man possessed, strike the fiend down! Woe to us in our innocence, consign the conqueror to the earth.

THE MAN *convulsions, singing with a bleeding, visible wound* Senseless desire from horror to horror, Insatiable gyration in the void. Labor without birth, sunfall, heaving space. End of those who praised me. O, your pitiless word!

WARRIORS *to the Man* We know him not. Spare us! Come you Greek maidens, let us unite in wedlock on the bed of his plight.

ALL MAIDENS He puts us in fear, you we loved, when you came.
The Maidens join the Men on the ground on the right, caressing. Three warriors make a stretcher of ropes and branches and put it in the tower, with the Man, who is still making slight movements, on it. Women slam the barred gate shut and return to join the men.

THE OLD MAN *rises and locks it. All dark, a little light in the cage.*

THE WOMAN *alone, moaning, defiant* He cannot live, cannot die, He is completely white.
She prowls round the cage. Reaches out compulsively toward the bars. Shakes her fist.

THE WOMAN *defiantly* Open the door, I must go to him!
Shakes the bars in despair.

WARRIORS AND WOMEN *amused, in the shadows, jumble of voices* We've lost the key — we'll find it — Have you got it? — did you see it? *To the Man and Woman* We are not to blame. We do not

know you — What do we know of you! Your quarrel makes no sense and has been going on for ever.
They go back. A cock crows; it gets lighter in the background.

THE WOMAN *putting her arm in through the bars, gasping with malevolence* Pale man! Do you flinch? Do you know fear? Are you merely sleeping? Are you awake? Do you hear me?

THE MAN *inside, breathing heavily, raises his head with a great effort, later moves one hand, then both hands, slowly stands up, singing, becoming ecstatic* Wind that blows, time after time. Solitude, rest, and hunger confuse me. Worlds circling by, no air, evening grows long.

THE WOMAN *beginnings of fear* So much life flowing out of the crack, So much strength out of the door, Pale as a corpse he is.

Creeps up the steps again, her whole body quivering, laughing out loud once more.

The Man has slowly stood up, leans against the bars.

THE WOMAN *growing weaker, in fury* In this cage I am taming a wild beast, Is your song baying with hunger?

The Man opens his mouth to speak.
A cock crows

THE WOMAN *quivering* You — are not dying?

THE MAN *powerfully* Stars and moon! Woman! Brightly shining, in dream or awake, I saw a singing being . . . Breathing, a darkness unravels. Mother . . . You lost me here.

The Woman is lying fully on him, separated by the bars; slowly she opens the door.

THE WOMAN *softly* Do not forget me . . .

THE MAN *wiping his eyes* The rust of thoughts clings to my forehead . . .

THE WOMAN *tenderly* It is your wife!

THE MAN *gently* A brief span of timid light! —

THE WOMAN *pleading* Man!! Sleep, for my sake . . .

THE MAN *louder* Quiet, quiet, delusion, let me . . .
The Woman opens her mouth to speak

THE MAN *solitary* I am afraid —

THE WOMAN *more and more violently, crying out* I cannot let you live. Man! You weaken me — I will kill you — You shackle me! I took you captive — and you hold me! Let go of me — clasping me — as if with chains of iron — throttling me — let go — help! I lost the key — which held you fast.
Lets go of the bars, collapses on the steps.

The Man standing erect, tears open the door, touches the woman, who, rearing up, rigid, has gone all white, with the fingers of his outstretched hand. She feels her end coming, tenses her limbs, and releases them in a single, slowly diminishing cry. The Woman falls down dead; falling she pulls the torch out of the hand of the Old Man as he stands up; the torch goes out, enveloping everything in a shower of sparks.

The man stands on the top step, Warriors and Maidens, trying to flee from him, run screaming into his path.

WARRIORS AND MAIDENS The Devil! Tie him down! Run! Everyone for himself — lost!

The man goes straight toward them. He swats them like flies. The flames spread to the tower and rip it open from the bottom to the top. The Man rushes off down the passage through the fire. A long way off a cock crows.

SPHINX AND STRAWMAN

An Oddity

(Published version, in: Oskar Kokoschka, *Dramen und Bilder*, Kurt Wolff Verlag, Leipzig, 1913.)

Sphinx and Strawman, An Oddity

CHARACTERS

HUGH AVVER *a gigantic revolving straw head with arms and legs, carrying a pig's bladder on a string*
INDIARUBBERMAN *an educated contortionist*
FEMALE SOUL *called 'Anima'*
DEATH *a normal living person*

Sphinx and Strawman, An Oddity   41

AVVER *waggling his head on his legs, to the parrot* Who are you, what are you called?

PARROT   The female soul, Anima, sweet Anima.

AVVER *turning aside* I had a wife, I made a god of her, and she left my bed. Said to her sorrowing lady's maid, "Tie my traveling veil for me," and disappeared with a healthy muscleman. I created a human soul, and the ground disappeared from under its feet. And my creation hangs in the air like a pig's bladder. — Nature abhors a vacuum!
Who is the god who steals the words out of my mouth, so that I might believe he taught me them? Just as a sponge soaks up vinegar and discharges it without having swallowed the least drop?

PARROT   Anima, sweet Anima!

AVVER   At first it was a woman, and then I was dining with a mask, sharing the thrill of coitus with a specter, and solving the puzzles of a phenomenon of the vocal cords. A nightmare sat down on my head, strangling my consciousness. O vitality, essentiality, reality, help me!
Woe to the Adonis whom she will spiritualize until he begins to speak with my tongues. A woman who gave her maidenhead for a soul is now going from one man to another, spinning herself into a cocoon, eating the men's skulls bare, and leaving them just once as a magnificent butterfly, simply in order to lay her egg. Anima, Anima, one supplied the nucleus, another protoplasm, and we all recognize ourselves in the thing she gave birth to. Resurrection from the living. I want to die.

Amid thunder and lightning Death appears as a normal person, smiling, he wags a warning finger and disappears without doing anything.

AVVER *to the audience* How touching, when I take out a handkerchief, you start to cry. Why are you giving me those cool looks now, a hundred indifferent people to one excited man. A mere nuance distinguishing the hero from the audience.
Do you think I'm bluffing?
The only things I work with are your intelligence, your nerves, and the results of our mutual Romantic belief in ghosts.

INDIARUBBERMAN *appears, touches him on the leg* Hello, hello, hello, I'm a doctor. You want to die! We can discuss this, can't we, an interchange of views does not take place simply to exchange interviews, but with a view to change? Dying's not as easy as being born.
If it's your last hour that happens to be causing you problems, I have a solution. I observe a woman . . .
Anima peeps in at the door
who is slowly killing her husband, without the courts being able to prove a thing to the world at large. "Fear of adultery" is a poison that is dead certain in its effect. Interested?

AVVER Thanks, but no . . .
lost in thought
things aren't that bad yet . . . I think . . .
But you're a doctor, shouldn't you be preventing crime?

INDIARUBBERMAN It's experiments that interest me. I'm not a family doctor, I'm just a humble priest of science.

ANIMA *in a low voice* A man, greatness and humility, and me so fascinated by anything striking.

AVVER *embarrassed, pulls a rubber doll over his finger and makes it nod* Allow me to perform the introductions: My child, Emmanuel, my hope — Mr. Indiarubberman!

INDIARUBBERMAN See you're a credit to your father, Master Emmanuel, me young youknowwhat. *To Avver* But permit me to remark, purely as a matter of information, that, in order to validate the birth of your offspring according to the ruling of the ruling class, proof of at least his most important progenitors must be established.

AVVER *confused, pulls the doll off his finger* Oh my dear sir, please don't express yourself so freely, my child is still innocent. But you are right. The fact that he had no mother could hold up Emmanuel's progress.

PARROT Anima, sweet Anima.

ANIMA *light blue, the usual angel's costume, wings, hands together, goes up to the two men* God, if only I could save the soul of a man, too, they say they suffer so from the mysteries of their sophisticated erotic conventions.
Pointing to Indiarubberman
You ought to be dignified, you have powerful muscles.
Pleased, Indiarubberman ripples his thigh muscles. She looks coquettishly down at her own little feet which are turned out, one to the front, one more to the back
Oh, terrible, don't you think, that one little foot is shorter than the other?

INDIARUBBERMAN *gallantly* The invention of perspective, merely an optical fraud by art historians.

ANIMA *relieved* It will give me a limp for all my born days. *Gathers up her dress a little and gives Avver, who has been ignoring her, a poke in the backside with her elegant foot.*

AVVER *grumbling* One should only look down on women.

Slowly turns his head, without moving his body. Step by step Anima keeps moving out of Avver's line of sight, until his head is back-to-

front on his body; in spite of vigorous efforts, he cannot manage to get it back into the traditional position. Thus Anima remains unknown to Avver right up to the end.
Plaintively If one shows consideration and respect when making love, the indignant Amazons are not sufficiently aroused; if, on the other hand, one is rough and imperious, it gives a shock to our own sensitive nerves.
Walking backwards to the door, rings for the servant John, bring a mirror, a red rose, and the photographer. Put the cockatoo in the pink room.
The servant brings the rose and the mirror.
Avver strides back to the chair in his practiced backward walk, sits down the wrong way round, tries to stick the rose into his back, then, finally, into his necktie, looks at his behind in the mirror, then his face.

ANIMA *has changed her clothes, sophisticated opulence, a book in her hand, sings* Oh where is he who would be worthy of me, of whom I dreamt as a girl; as he did, no man yet has proved himself to me. One trait I took from one, one in another note of, to my lover I proffered resigned lips, to my husband mocking melancholy. Doomed to shuttle between the twain, from one to the other, then back again.
to Avver Good morning, handsome.

AVVER *without being able to see her* Who are you, what are you called? Angel.

ANIMA The female soul, Anima, sweet Anima.

PARROT *mimicking her* Anima, sweet Anima.

AVVER *pulling a face as if he were at the dentist's* This was my doom once before. Women have an earthly body, but an immortal soul.

Sphinx and Strawman, An Oddity 45

ANIMA *pointing at his figure* That's an interesting view. *Avver assumes she means his remark, blows out his manly chest in pride.*

ANIMA Oh, I feel I love only you.

AVVER *grotesquely grandiloquent* Alone and abandoned, to quiver in expectation of your secret confessions, to set the rainbow of reconciliation over the shocked sexes.
Cracking up My feelings are like fixed stars falling from the sky, whizzing into the enclosed fields of my soul, there to die out — but the word, reaching out beyond me like a gesture, is for you nothing but an anemic device.

ANIMA Oh, but I'm passionately fond of devices! Oh, my big, sweet head. My light, my truth. *Jumping into his arms with a screech* My lord and master, sweet Mr. Avver.

AVVER My self-confidence is rising!

Indiarubberman is breathing heavily, Anima touches the tip of his nose with her foot, Indiarubberman quivers with tender emotion.

ANIMA *softly* Oh Mr. Indiarubberman, I think I'm in love, but I'm not certain. Do you two gentlemen know each other — Indiarubberman.

AVVER *automatically introducing himself* Hugh Avver.

INDIARUBBERMAN With the greatest of pleasure. *A very bizarre, low bow; because of his organic shortcomings, when Avver bows, his head goes away from Indiarubberman.*

AVVER Emmanuel is going to have a mother!

PARROT Anima, sweet Anima!

46 *Sphinx and Strawman, An Oddity*

Death appears, 'mid thunder and lightning, Avver filled with terror

AVVER *screaming* Entreprise des pompes funèbres! Rapists and murderers über alles. The thought of a future makes the present coagulate.

AVVER *looking for Anima* I don't even have a photograph of her.

DEATH *knocking on the proscenium arch with a bone. Avver gets pains in his limbs*
In order to reassure the audience, I would like to point out, even though it spoils the effect of the theatrical device, that Death has lost his terror since the male imagination in Europe has become completely tied down by gynolatry.

AVVER *apprehensively, but more calmly* The human soul is like a magic lantern — it used to show the writing on the wall, now it projects our women onto the world.
Quivering like a galvanized eel, bursts the pig's bladder That was the soul, that was.
Resigned Oh I'll never believe no fairy tales again, instead I'll have a little laugh.
Smiles, louder, resonance of a hundred voices, torrential echo, simply soothing
My technique for restoring my bodily balance.
Tightens his trouser-belt and is pursued by Death. Anima screams, flees into the pink room with Indiarubberman. Avver tries to follow, groping, but cannot find the right direction.. Meanwhile the pink room lights up, two shadows kissing.

PARROT O my Anima, sweet Anima.
Distinctly O my sweet Mr. Indiarubberman! O my sweet Mr. Indiarubberman! O my sweet Mr. Indiarubberman!

Sphinx and Strawman, An Oddity

AVVER *as a result of the unaccustomed supplement to the parrot's cry, his head snaps back into place; he sees the shadows, rushes to the telephone* Who are you?

ANIMA Anima, your sweet Anima, the female soul.

AVVER What are you up to?

ANIMA Spiritualist experiments, conjuring up spirits. I'm going to get myself redeemed.

AVVER Who am I?

PARROT O my sweet Mr. Indiarubberman!
Avver staggers to the center of the stage, lies down flat on the floor, and shoots himself with an air pistol. Horns grow on his head.
John pulls up a curtain from under the pink room, on which a huge cat catching a mouse has been painted. Underneath are painted a number of men, dressed in black, with top hats and, instead of faces, holes, in which for a brief time a head appears and quickly speaks one of the following lines, to which the next man responds, the conversation going in this way along the whole line.

FIRST MAN The Enlightenment will have poor progeny, their brains are too heavy — and their hips too light-headed.

SECOND MAN They lack the stabilizing influence of a conscience.

THIRD MAN Death has handed over his power to a woman.

FOURTH MAN Thus a respected fantast brings the miracles of culture down to earth.

FIFTH MAN Avver, who is said to be descended from a woman, has given his birthright, his male imagination, back to his wife, and now her soul is suffering.

SIXTH MAN He persuaded a woman who was in labor to put the fetus she had aborted into her mouth and believed she would give birth to it.

SEVENTH MAN That invention, o humanity, is the mother of necessity.

EIGHTH MAN Can modern science not help?

NINTH MAN Science has gone coy since people in kindergarten know her progenitor.

TENTH MAN Man must be happy to suffer the torments woman causes him, for he can *understand* the reasons for which she lives a different life from him. In his wisdom, he replaces "it is" with the better "it could be," and in that way rounds off his range of experience.

ANIMA *comes rushing up to Avver, in tears.*

AVVER *making his final effort* I forgot! — A priest!

INDIARUBBERMAN *following Anima, no tie* What about the wedding?
Singing Give lust its head, conscience is dead.
Eugenics, eugenics, let the tender passion be consummated before the eyes of scientists.

AVVER *making his absolutely final effort* Passion needs the spirit as a filter, otherwise it will flood body and soul, polluting both. I believe in the genius of humanity, Anima, amen.

DEATH *with thunder and lightning* Honest faith is like blindness. It throws a veil over unpleasant things, without them for that reason disappearing.

Death exits with Anima, whom he tries to comfort, with every sign of success.

SPHINX AND STRAWMAN

A Comedy for Mechanical Dolls

(From the manuscript, first published in *Wort in der Zeit*, vol. 2, 1956, part 3. Performed in 1907 on the stage of the Academy for Applied Arts, Vienna, and at the Kokoschka Matinée, 29 March, 1909 in the "Fledermaus" revue theater, Vienna.)

Sphinx and Strawman for Mechanical Dolls

CHARACTERS

HUGH AVVER
INDIARUBBERMAN
LILLY
NINE MEN AT THE WEDDING RECEPTION
DEATH AND PRIEST
PHOTOGRAPHER
COCKATOO

Sphinx and Strawman for Mechanical Dolls   53

AVVER *enormous, revolving, straw-colored, gigantic head; evening dress; sorrowful; rocking in a wicker chair with a cockatoo on his finger* Cockatoo, you rock me like an African wind, you sad head-hanger. My Lilly said serenely to her sorrowing lady's maid, "Find my hairpins, you silly goose," and left with an Adonis of a bodyman *to the audience* according to reliable reports. Why are you giving me such cool looks? A thousand indifferent faces to one, *pointing to himself* still, a nuance distinguishing the actor from the audience. *Casually* Do you think I'm trying to fool you — the only things I work with are our homespun intelligence, our nerves, and the results of the Romantic belief in psychological ghosts we share.

INDIARUBBERMAN *enters, top hat, bright red face, contortionist* Hello, hello, hello, let's discuss things — an interchange of views does not take place simply to exchange interviews, but with a view to change, don't you agree?

AVVER *nods dreamily, takes a rubber doll, the kind you put on your thumb, out of his pocket, kisses it tenderly and introduces it to Indiarubberman* My son Adam, my hope — Mr. Indiarubberman.

INDIARUBBERMAN *gasping for breath, returning the doll's bow once he has finished coughing* See you're a credit to your father, my young youknowwhat. *to Avver* But permit me to remark, purely as a matter of information, that, in order to validate the birth of an offspring, proof of the existence of its minimally indispensable progenitors must be established, according to the ruling of the ruling class.

AVVER *confused, puts his son back in his pocket, embarrassed* Oh my dear sir, please don't express yourself so freely, my son is still innocent, *reflectively* but you are right, my son ought to have a mother. *bursting out sobbing* Heartless Lilly! *to the audience, casually* How touching the way those people down there are ready to respond. I only have to take out my handkerchief and already they're crying.

LILLY *swaying her hips as she walks, made up to the nines, singing, hands reverently together* God, if only I could save the heart of a man, they say they suffer so from the mysteries of their sophisticated erotic conventions. *pointing to Indiarubberman* You ought to be dignified, you have powerful muscles. *pleased, Indiarubberman ripples his thigh muscles. She looks coquettishly down at her own little feet which are turned out, one to the front, one more to the back* Oh, terrible, don't you think, that one little foot is shorter than the other?

INDIARUBBERMAN *gallantly* An invention of perspective, merely an optical fraud by art historians.

LILLY *relieved* It will give me a limp for all my born days. *Gathers up her dress a little and gives Avver, who has been ignoring her, a poke in the backside with her sweet, elegant foot.*

AVVER *grumbling* One should only look down on women. *slowly turns his head, without moving his body. Step by step, Lilly keeps moving out of Avver's line of sight, until his head is back-to-front on his body; in spite of vigorous efforts, he cannot manage to get it back into the traditional position. Thus Lilly remains unknown to Avver right up to the end.*
Plaintively If one is timid and tender when making love, the indignant Amazons do not feel sufficiently understood; if, on the other hand, one is rough and imperious, it gives a shock to our own sensitive nerves.*walking backwards to the door, rings for the servant* John, bring a mirror, a red rose, and the photographer. Put the cockatoo in the bedroom.

Servant brings the things he asked for. The couple exchange rings. The photographer takes a picture of the couple in a very dignified wedding pose. He'll bring the prints tomorrow.

AVVER *strides back to the chair in his practiced backward walk, sits down the wrong way round, backwards, forwards, finally making do with the floor, looks at his back in the mirror, then his bald head, finally finds his face, first tries to stick the rose into his back, then, finally, into his buttonhole.*

LILLY *has changed her dress, a dachshund on a silk lead, bored, sings as she enters*
    My little dog's called Fritz the Prussian,
    no man ever understood me like he,
    to my lover I proffered resigned lips
    to my husband mocking melancholy.
    — — — Hello, handsome.
AVVER *speaking to the pocket where Adam is kept* She and no other will become your mother. *John appears* What is your name, enigmatic angel?

LILLY Lilly.

AVVER *pulling a face as if he were at the dentist's* That name was my doom once before. *She is drumming on his bald pate; he is partly pleased, partly suffering from dismal memories* Women are ghosts, they live on in us, even after you're divorced. Our lovers have immortal souls but no hearts.

LILLY You have such interesting views. *She means the odd way he is put together, he assumes she means his intelligence, blows out his manly chest.*

AVVER Oh, I feel I will have to love her. Alone and abandoned, to quiver in expectation of her secret confessions, to set the rainbow of reconciliation over the shocked sexes. *with inward grandiloquence* My feelings are like rockets, falling to be extinguished in the firmly fenced-off fields of my soul — the word, reaching out beyond them like a gesture, is for her nothing but a bloodless device.

LILLY Oh, but I'm passionately fond of devices!
Oh, my sweet red beard,
my flame *jumping into his arms with a screech*
Oh, savior of my body, sweet Mr. Avver!

AVVER Oh, my sweet, sweet Lilly!

Indiarubberman comes up, breathing heavily, Lilly, still clinging to Avver, taps him on the nose with the tip of her toe; amorous buttock-vibrato

LILLY Oh, the fat man's come, do you gentlemen know each other? Mr. Indiarubberman, my fiancé — —

AVVER *automatically giving his name, unaware of the double meaning* Hugh Avver.

INDIARUBBERMAN I have already had the pleasure. *a very bizarre, low bow; because of his organic shortcomings, when Avver bows, his head goes away from Indiarubberman*

AVVER Excuse me a second, darling. *blows a little trumpet* John, invite some guests to the wedding. *Lilly with Indiarubberman. Death and Priest — arm in arm, serious, crooked — come in through the door; Avver terrified, screams*
   Entreprise de pompes funèbres!
   Rapists and murderers über alles!
   Like strong onions
   They draw the tears from my cheeks.
With a cry, Lilly flees into the house, Indiarubberman following her

AVVER *groping after Lilly* I don't even have a photograph of her.

DEATH *knocking with his knuckle on the proscenium arch. Avver gets toothache* In order to reassure the public I would like to point out, even though it spoils the artistic effect, that there are no real dead people here, nor will there be. *exit*

AVVER *apprehensively* Human society is like a magic lantern: it used to make God and the Devil appear on the wall, as if by magic — and today it's the ghosts of our own souls. *quivers like a galvanized eel; sudden transformation* I'm going to have a little laugh. *smiles, louder, with a thousand voices, isolated, sweeping torrential echo, fifteen seconds, calming, simple* My technique for restoring my spiritual balance. *tightens his trouser-belt and retires. John covers the wall with a curtain, on which a gigantic cat catching a mouse is painted together with nine top hats and nine black suits with holes between them through which, as the dialogue begins, the nine men slowly stick their heads and then withdraw them.*

ALL NINE MEN *loudly* Bonsoir, chers amis *above the nine wedding guests two windows of the pink room are visible; pink light, two shadows kissing.*

INDIARUBBERMAN Oh, my sweet Lilly!

LILLY Oh, my sweet Mr. Indiarubberman!

both of the above slowly repeated three times

COCKATOO *mimicking* Oh, my sweet Lilly!
Oh my sweet Mr. Indiarubberman!

Cockatoo slowly repeats three times.

During the above scene and taking up the same amount of time, the men stick their heads through the holes, in the manner of mechanical dolls, rattle off a sentence in a shrill voice and disappear amid a stench.

FIRST MAN Rrrsss! It's really funny that healthy lads with no complexes are usually stuck in a dead end, while weaklings rule the world. Ffsssh. *off; Cockatoo*

SECOND MAN *to the third* Cooooee! — — — noble sentiments, memories of puberty, when I failed to solve a problem in the school of love. I couldn't answer the Sphinx's question. — — —

THIRD MAN hhhummmmm, and me even more in celibacy, when my instincts did headstands like well-trained poodles. — — — Brrr. —

FOURTH MAN For example: women are sphinxes made of scented flounces, manicured fingertips, and delicate details.

FIFTH MAN Or a man's love is the synthesis of woman.

SIXTH MAN Are you afraid of the world beyond — — —?

SEVENTH MAN If it's beyond the audience.

EIGHTH MAN rrrtch boommmmm *there is a sudden explosion as he is about to speak; trembling with fear, nine faces appear several times — synchronized — in the holes, then disappear. The shadows kiss, Cockatoo repeats itself furiously, Avver comes downstage, attentive, listens, turns round, sees Lilly for the first time and Indiarubberman. The photographer brings the wedding photograph. Avver sees and hears. Screams and kicks his feet.*

AVVER I have married my own wife.

NINTH MAN *at lightning speed* By day sex is silent, but in the night the cry of shame of the youngest girl and the oldest graybeard echoes in our ears. *the pink room goes dark, Lilly and Indiarubberman rush out bewildered, bawling.*

LILLY *bawling* I believe my dear fiancé has just gone to meet his Maker. — Clear his mortal remains away. *steps over the dead body as beautifully as a parade-ground horse* I will live on without him.

JOB

A Drama (1917)

Dedicated to Fritz Neuberger in sincere friendship

Job

CHARACTERS

JOB
ANIMA, his wife
INDIARUBBERMAN
ADAM, the gardener
EROS
LADY'S MAID
YOUNG LADIES
MEN
PARROT

Motto: Bone of contention

While Adam was sleeping on the green grass,
God took pity, the sun was right overhead
And He was close to sleeping from the ennui.
Cried Adam, in the night by a rib-roaster roused, "Ah me!"
Then, finding himself coupled with Eve, said,
"My God, if he'd only left my rib in peace."

ACT ONE

JOB *in nightcap and dressing gown, knocks at the door to his wife's room*

LADY'S MAID *cautiously putting her head round the other door, hiding something behind her back*
I knocked before, I've a favor to ask.
Could Sir help me get something off
My back?
With a couple of kicks, Madam applied it
To the small of my back; it comes garnished
With feathers and claws, tongue and beak.
Madam herself went out this morning
With the young gentleman, he's as pretty as a picture.
This feathered friend she left for Sir
To amuse himself with.
Throws a parrot out of a basket. The parrot flies onto Job's shoulder.

LADY'S MAID *exits, warbling*
It is the balmy summer's eve —
It disappeared, and sighs from
A deep cleft in the earth.
Waters tongues, sours tears —
Weaves and spins, behind a nightlight,

its net,the lock of blond hair —
Catches the heroes, drawn by danger . . .

JOB
And I thought she was here just now?
pointing at the door
Bartered her maidenhead for a soul —
Slipping from one man to another,
And leaving the skull when it's eaten bare,
pointing to his forehead
Here, where she nested, as she flew
Off she quickly laid an egg,
From out of which she'll skip, a phoenix, young once more. —
I don't want to have a sun rising,
No skies building up, with
Castles in the air, and sphinxes conversing
Outside! . . .
Walks up and down; with one bound, Parrot leaps onto his head
Woe to the youth she thinks to spiritualize
Until with my tongue he speaks and replies.
Sinking into a chair
Once, long ago, from the creator's head
Sprang the mother of creation,
His world concealed within her womb.
Parrot tousles his hair
Hey — hey, my head!
Where did it go so soon?
Oh, nature abhors a vacuum!
Sings
How love has twisted me
Since in this empty house
A voice sweetly laden, of a young maiden,
Called me to seek her out.
— A labyrinth is tormenting me,
From which echos tease,
Set me scampering here and there at every breeze.

As you sow, so shall you reap.
I love her so, she leads me up the garden path,
And nothing do I reap
Because, at that moment, swiftly,
She's transforming herself through some loophole
Into a being that — I am myself!

ANIMA *outside the door, sings*

JOB *doesn't hear her, plays with the bird, lures it onto his finger*
What gives a man the time of his life?

PARROT *imitating the female voice*
Anima — your soul, your wife.

JOB
My soul!
Her rudeness or flight or whatever I
Should call it, leaves me
With the thought that . . . but . . .
Is there a name a man calls his own?

PARROT
Is there an aim? — man all alone!
The parrot jumps back onto Job's head, ruffles his hair in friendly fashion

JOB
That two-faced woman has gone to my head —
Speaks with my lips
Peeks out of my eyes
Pumps me. Pumps me dry!
Shaking his importunate squatter, which holds onto his ears
I'll be like a pumpkinhead shortly,
Putrefying in the pit with its
Spectral glow.

The bird spreads itself out on Job's head and bloats itself up
Hope or spite,
You are getting too heavy!
Leave me a clear head,
So I can bear you.
I'll grab you!
Help!
more softly
But isn't that her speaking? How . . .?

ANIMA *echoing*
I cannot relieve you —
United we are!
Ever — One.

JOB
But, in heaven's name — or hell's —
Tell me now — who you are!

ANIMA *echoing*
Anima it is, your wife! I am your soul!

JOB
Gone is — I am — and what about — me?
In despair, he rattles the doorhandle again
I had a wife,
She was my world!
In tears
I thought to embrace the rim
Of the globe, when the ground
Disappeared from under my feet, and
My lordship was left hanging like a —
Pig's bladder in the air!
Nature abhors a vacuum!
Steadying himself
Though it was only a plan.

Still it was my world!
Dizzy, stumbles

ANIMA *from behind the door, gently*
If you don't take care,
Too boldly dare,
You can lose your head!

JOB *irritated*
Head! World! One's the same as the other!
The words are being taken
Out of my mouth!
I want to believe I'm being taught
Something new!
As a sponge soaks up vinegar,
Releases it without swallowing . . .
Outraged, he turns away from the door, after his attempts to gain entrance there are in vain

ANIMA *softly* . . . A man, of course,
Should not ask me to dine,
Who gave vinegar and wanted wine.

ACT TWO

JOB *flees, in order to be alone, to the upstairs drying-room, where ladies' and gentlemen's underwear is hung up on lines to dry. Clambers up to the skylight. Outside it's blowing a gale with thunder and lightning. About to throw himself out, he notices something in the street.*
O ye elements! Pour forth, heavens!
Surge, drench this agitated breast!
A dog . . .! Here, boy!
A faithful hound . . .
Last solace for one to whom mankind
Is hateful.

THE POODLE *runs in through the vestibule, opens the door, jumps up at Job, wagging its tail*
Bow-wow . . . Bow-wow,
A dog has a keen nose
I'm a psychologist!
How now? . . . How now?
A thorn that's lost its rose!

INDIARUBBERMAN *wriggling out of the poodle's skin*
Excuse the silly disguise —
I'm the kernel of the cur,
As a poet once said.
You've become something of a hermit.
Points to the vestibule
But the nice maid down there would
Not turn a dog away
When it's raining cats and dogs!
Hats off to a man
Whose very vitals are churned up by feeling.
The day it flags — off with his head!
It is true that research has shown that the heart,
For a while after the decapitation of a

Condemned man, still beats full of feeling.
What has not been shown so far is
Whether the feelings are all pleasant.
However much it is wound up,
Every clock runs down some time.
As I had occasion to remark in a
Different form — I'm a psychologist and employ
Myself usefully giving good advice.
Life's advocate I did not become,
It can kill the patient itself.
Trust me, and that'll give
Me a claim on you.
Don't you agree? To exchange views
Is not to review exchanges
But is done with a view to changes.
Out of the window Indiarubberman sees the lady of the house return, who then busies herself in the next room. Full of curiosity, he snoops at the keyhole. At the movements coming from the next room Job turns away sulkily and stiffly.
What a beauty!
Taking my fancy — and her clothes off!
To Job, who can only stop himself from looking at the ominous door with the greatest difficulty
By the way, should her *accouchement*,
Which is drawing nigh,
Require a *diligence* . . .
Strenuously concentrating on the keyhole, almost crawling into it
I am observing a woman who,
To put it briefly, is
Wringing a man's neck!

JOB *indignantly, standing to one side*
. . . And you, a doctor, the
Friend of the weak, are doing nothing
To prevent this act of violence?

70   *Job*

INDIARUBBERMAN Only out of private scientific interest.
I'm sorry — I'm not a doctor
To the door
. . . it's experiments that interest me . . .
Delighted
. . . Eureka! I've got it! . . . Her means! . . . Discovered!
— Eroditis, jealousy! The seed
Incubated by Erotococcus,
a bacillus that people call the witches' dart!
My colleagues left that for me
To discover! That's what's done it
In your case, where the patient,
Weakened by long suffering,
Is no longer immune.

ANIMA *from the adjoining room*
Easily can Science headless render
The man who does not fit its rules.
It cuts him off from his head, the man who, by ideas,
By the power of God or love, perplexed, perverted,
Lost in thought for a while, turns his back on his own little ego.

Job sees how Indiarubberman, drooling and with a lascivious eye, is glued to the keyhole. The door opens slowly, Anima comes out, stops; Job, driven mad by the sight, turns his face away and cannot get his head back into the traditional position; he clutches his ears in horror, tears out great tufts of hair.

INDIARUBBERMAN *runs over to Job, horrified*
Here, let me feel your pulse.
The man's dying on me in a state of fright!
You're suffocating! Loosen your collar!
You're doing everything wrong!
Your affliction comes from your
Twisted view of things which can't
Be straightened out.

JOB *bellowing*
Someone's turned my head!
My body's going off my head!
Whimpers
Off my head!

INDIARUBBERMAN *fussing about Job's chest*
His heart is still sound! I have to
Stop the double circulation
Taking out a surgical saw
So that the infection will not
Paralyze his heart. Off with your head!
Chin up! Headless, your ailment will not
Be half so bad!

ANIMA
My God, if only I could
Help! No one's paying any attention to me.

JOB *dancing round in circles, bellowing to keep Indiarubberman away, who is waving his saw about*
I think I must be losing
My head!
Does this one belong to me . . . that one?
You are closest to me . . . that
Means . . . I must get my hands
Round your throat!
I grasp — I seize!
I fall — I release!
shattered
To be a mere reflection,
The shape of something all eyes see.
To Indiarubberman
Why are you gawping at me so calmly,
Just you wait,
One calm man — against a deranged one!

72 *Job*

Tries to tear his head off his shoulders, beats his forehead with his fist
A world projected — rejected!
The globe turns . . . rolls away!
That woman has bewitched . . . turned
My head . . . it is possessed!

INDIARUBBERMAN *inviting Anima to come closer while he studies Job's head*
If a woman possesses her husband's
Head, she will try to find herself a
Lover in exchange for it.
And since I take an interest in hers . . .
Ah, here she comes . . .
Do please introduce me.

ANIMA *innocent, respectable, gentle, blond*
You wicked man! You're scolding me!
Me! Anima! Your wife!
Of the breath, which blew life into creation —
From which impatience drove out
Anima before fulfillment.

JOB *holding out his hands in an imploring gesture*
Anima, my soul!

PARROT *flies into the room, squawking*
Anima! My soul!

JOB *stretching out his arm to try and catch Anima, who turns to Indiarubberman*
Escaped from my head, with him! —
Together with the soul of sleepy Adam!

INDIARUBBERMAN *pulling Anima to his breast*
That bit in the Bible about the old potter?
No, woman was not made from your clay!

EROS *tripping in through the door, saucy*
From Father's tears there sprang in
Mother's womb a little boy . . .

ANIMA *bitterly; Eros stumbles, blubbers and rubs his leg*
Bringing joy, so the mother of sorrows thought!

INDIARUBBERMAN
I don't understand a word!
Ha! What joy to be alive! . . .

From now on all crashing about in chaos, shouting, parrot squawking on and on, Eros howling

JOB *trying to calm the child down. To Indiarubberman*
Opportunist!
What she thought a springboard, along which, from
one pleasure to another, to vault,
Oh gross clay, ever billing and cooing! Each of its
seven heavens an inferno!
The little creature fell, as it came down to earth,
And is already crying at the door.

INDIARUBBERMAN *to Job*
It's the spitting image of you.
But teach the squalling brat to stop chattering.
Everything in this house is haunted.
To the lady's maid, pointing at the parrot
Throw the noisy beast out.

JOB
To hell with it, where it came from!

ANIMA *taking Eros by the hands and dancing round with him and out of the door*
To hell with hell, to hell with heaven!
My darling is Eros, the god.
With imagination I gave birth to him —
Of whom I dreamt even as a little girl.
One trait I took from one man,
One in another note of.
To my lover I proffered resigned lips,
To my husband mocking melancholy.
From One to the Other! As a bee
Slips gathering! Till Eros the god arrived!

INDIARUBBERMAN *bellows, since the noise has subsided, at the fleeing pair*
But, dear lady . . . stay . . .
Your Eros stimulates me too! . . .
Allow me the purely factual observation
That I feel moved by the genesis
Of your mythological boy
To seek a natural explanation.

ACT THREE

Job has fallen asleep from his cares on a bench outside his house. The little garden is planted with little blossom trees.

FIRST YOUNG LADY *her curly head quietly emerging from the rosebed, tries to wake Job and to grasp his hand, which is hanging down*
Just as you like it!
My God! In the wilderness
The strong eat the weak.
In society it's vice versa!
That often gives one the face
Of a sheep, the lethargy of a capon and . . .

JOB *softly, in his sleep*
. . . and you the brain of a chicken.

SECOND YOUNG LADY *softly, laughing behind a tree*
. . . Yes! Whenever a young hothead
Comes to visit her,
She jumps straight into bed.
She begs his pardon, but —
He has to have a red coxcomb!

THIRD YOUNG LADY *crouching under the bench, softly, looking up to him*
You won't throw him
Off balance any more!
There he is, homo anthropos!
Just feel those calves!

JOB *tickled, kicks out in his sleep, so that the young lady tumbles*

THIRD YOUNG LADY
Damned worm's-eye view!

76 *Job*

It'll give me a limp all my born days!

FOURTH YOUNG LADY *tickling Job's ear with a flower-stalk and dropping an apple; she is in a bush behind the bench*
If you ignore women,
You'll never make it to
Posterity!

JOB *dreaming*
When you think that
Posterity is made with the help of such good-for-nothing
Females,
You lose your belief in
A better future!

FIFTH YOUNG LADY *reaching out toward his hair from behind the drapes over the doorway; softly*
It's Dame Fortune. Grab hold.
Otherwise she'll take you all by the forelock!

SIXTH YOUNG LADY *gives him a pat on the back*
A man of breeding —
Just consider from which side
You want to show yourself!

JOB *sleepily*
That Dame Fortune is another
Of those elusive monkeys
Who would like her backside
Chased after.
As she's quick to bare it,
Take heed, which
Horn of plenty she may
Surprise you with!

SEVENTH YOUNG LADY *up in the tree, mocking*

To drift toward your
Secret confessions, to set
The rainbow of reconciliation
Over the warring sexes.

JOB *overwhelmed with melancholy, dreamily*
My feelings are meteors falling
From the sky, racing into the night
Of my own heart, there to be smothered!
— The word, that reaches out beyond me
Like the gesture of an invisible hand,
Is for you nothing but a theatrical device!

ALL YOUNG LADIES *singing softly*
Oh, we love devices, farces and tragedies at midnight;
Which banished sleep . . .

JOB *mumbling*
No longer a demon, throned on high, kicking me into the mire —
A gentle angel, cooling my brow?

EIGHTH YOUNG LADY
Look around, Sunday's child!
Ghosts do not wear clothes.
What harm can flesh and blood do?
*She comes from the path in the garden, which is now suffused with
a pale light; the sun rises, she kisses him on the forehead*
Good day, my friend,
Life is smiling upon you.

JOB *snarling at her, wiping off the kiss*
I've been struck by the witches' dart . . .

EIGHTH YOUNG LADY *gives him up*
The thought in an instant
Makes love curdle . . .

JOB *feeling himself front and back, to check whether something has happened to him again, staggers over to the light to see*

NINTH YOUNG LADY
Uprooted plants wither,
Whether they're in the shade or the light.

JOB *morosely*
Bottoms up, Dame Fortune,
Instead of the cock, the morning crows,
The game at the hunter looses arrows,
A weary man, cursing Carnival, shuts his windows.
Goes into the house. Brings a bottle of poison, a skull and two bones to the window, contemplates the skull, sets the bottle to his lips. The Tenth Young Lady reaches down from the tree and then beats a merry tattoo on the skull with the bones.

Job throws the bottle of poison at the Young Lady, who replies with the skull and bones, which Job wraps up in paper
You women, clear off, get lost!
closes the shutters
ALL THE YOUNG LADIES *disappear, softly singing the folk song*
Hush you bye,
Don't you cry
Go to sleepy, little baby . . .
Short pause

JOB *from behind the closed shutters*
The human soul or magic lantern . . .
It used to project God and the Devil onto the world,
Now it's women against a wall.
Humbly
To laugh just a little, to laugh . . .
And to stop running to the nursemaids, who give us children a tug.
The witch's at the window looking in, she's unmistakable.

He gives a soft smile, a silvery, many-voiced choir is echoing — torrential laughter, a hurricane — a flood of laughing. Job jumps out of the window, tightens his trouser-belt, stops in surprise. On the upper floor, above Job, a window lights up with a pink light. Parrot flies down from the open window, flutters in pursuit of the fleeing Job, opens its eyes wide, attacks him, during the following does not let him away from the shelter of the house wall, along which Job runs up and down

A set of horns grows on Job's head, points on the horns. Every time he rushes past the lighted window, two shadows throw articles of clothing onto them, soon forming a complete wardrobe. Cuffs, collars, jackets, nightwear, and underclothes for a gentleman and a lady

JOB *manages to get his hand on the doorbell; in mortal fear he rings the entryphone*
For pity's sake! I'm terrified!
Help me, Anima! Redemption!
What are they doing to me?!

ANIMA *from the window*
Invocation of spirits — do you feel it too?
That's always been the thing to do . . .

ADAM *the gardener, comes out of the garden*
A woman's making a fool of him,
She's the one that turned his head.

ANIMA
It was my mother wit suggested that!
A broad-minded spirit today took me to wife,
Broke the spell on me, and I'm giving a hand!

JOB
The devil! He really can cast spells!

And bravely with kisses and vows he invokes Anima.
O, gaping hell! Most fugitive of witches! Enters into a contract, yields!
In demure confusion her breast and neck blush; she opens her heart,
Laying aside skirts and mystery; and gets into bed to join
In housewifely fashion with masculine authority . . .
What's happening to me? It's not I who resemble the antagonist,
Settling down there and then begetting! . . .

ANIMA *falls down, scantily dressed, from the window like a ripe apple, landing with her bottom on Job's head, which falls off with Anima — Job dies. From the window Indiarubberman continues to make a pointed assault on her virtue. Anima, reproachfully*
Certainly not! — Mr. Indiarubberman!

PARROT
Certainly Mr. Indiarubberman . . .

ADAM *gently*
Too high was the pedestal
On which you placed your wife.
Only now she has fallen can you
Get to the bottom of her.
Adam pulls down a curtain which conceals the house, garden, Job, and Anima, and on which ten men dressed in mourning are painted. Where the faces should be, are holes, through which an actor sticks his head when, in the following dialogue, it is the turn of that particular figure to speak.

PARROT *explodes and goes to heaven as a pink cloud*

ADAM *watching him go*
In paradise once that same bird
Whispered a warning to me.
I was busy picking apples,
Ignored his plea.

Sighs

ANIMA *enters, munching an apple*
My late Job was also keen
For the apple of knowledge, oh . . .

FIRST MAN *cockily*
As the apple was maggoty,
Eve let her husband have first bite.

ADAM
Quiet! Order there!
It's not your turn yet!
One at a time, please!
First you have to stick your head through.
But keep your feet still
Or you'll bring the wall down.
The movement makes Job's head roll out in front of the wall.
Anima bends over it, horrified, almost goes out of her mind

SECOND MAN
Dame Sphinx, who was ill rewarded
For bringing the philosopher into the world —
His head above all — into the dung-heap
That posed riddles — now she's also known as Mrs. Anima.
And she lacks the imagination
To get herself sorted out!

THIRD MAN
Divine madness was the reason for the creation.

FOURTH MAN
One should persuade the poor, seduced girl
To reabsorb her stillbirth.
Let us hope she may still give birth to it!

82   *Job*

INDIARUBBERMAN *coming forward shyly*
Modern science
will help!

FIFTH MAN
Gone coy in the kindergartens
Because of its origins,
Limits itself to analyzing creation,
To see if it was necessary.

ADAM *drags Job's body out from under the curtain and fits his head back on neatly. Giving Indiarubberman an angry look*
The doctor invented the disease,
The patient has to foot the bill.

SIXTH MAN *to Job, who is lying down, stage front, his arms spread wide*
Death, who really crucified you
With that woman,
Won't open up a hellhole again with hustle-kerfuffle

SEVENTH MAN *to the sixth*
In the hellhole a single ray refracted
Into the light of a thousand colors!
The dark ages are passing,
Yielding to enlightened times!

EIGHTH MAN
The daily round will not be benighted again!
It's do, phoenix humanity, and die!

ADAM *softly, looking after Job, puts a handful of earth on his breast*
Such a mass of flowers from a spadeful of earth.
May the earth be easy on you.

ANIMA
Is he dead?

ADAM *calmly*
No. Only his head; his heart and other things have just given up the ghost.

INDIARUBBERMAN *blubbering*
Humanity must be
Elevated by breeding!
Eugenics, eugenics!
Let copulation take place
Before the eyes of scientists!

NINTH MAN
Science which is not purified by the filter of the spirit
Steamrollers life and death, polluting both.

TENTH MAN *vigorously*
I believe in the genius of humanity!
Anima — amen!

ADAM *gently, turning off the stage lights*
Honest belief is a green eyeshade,
Veiling the light of the world for sore eyes!
The only good thing left for me to do
Is to blow out the light
So that it does not have to burn.
Exits with Anima

ANIMA *in the dark*
Perhaps Job could only feel the heavy cross.
I have seen with my own eyes,
How they covered me with shame here.
Perhaps it's just me slandering myself —
And Anima, who gave Job the heavy cross to bear,

Is — Eve.

Alternative version to the opening of Act Three:

FIRST YOUNG LADY *her curly head quietly emerging from the rosebed, tries to wake Job and to grasp his hand, which is hanging down*
Just as you like it!
My God! In the wilderness
The strong eat the weak.
At home it's vice versa!
That often gives one the face
Of a sheep, the lethargy of a capon and . . .

JOB *softly, in his sleep*
. . . and you the brain of a chicken.

SECOND YOUNG LADY *softly, laughing behind a tree*
. . . Yes! Whenever a young hothead
Comes to visit her,
She jumps straight into bed.
She begs his pardon, but —
He has to have a red coxcomb!

THIRD YOUNG LADY *crouching under the bench, softly, looking up to him*
You won't throw him
Off balance any more!
There he is, homo anthropos!
Just feel those calves!

JOB *tickled, kicks out in his sleep, so that the young lady tumbles over*

THIRD YOUNG LADY
Damned worm's-eye view!
It'll give me a limp all my born days!

FOURTH YOUNG LADY *tickling Job's ear with a flower-stalk; she drops an apple, she is in a bush behind the bench*
Adam made it to
Posterity because he bowed before Eve in paradise

JOB *dreaming*
When you think that
Posterity is made with the help of such useless
pranks,
You lose your belief in
A better future!

FIFTH YOUNG LADY *reaching out toward his hair from behind the drapes over the doorway*
It's Dame Fortune. Grab hold.
Otherwise she'll take you all by the forelock!

SIXTH YOUNG LADY *gives him a pat on the back*
A man of breeding
Just consider from which side
You want to show yourself!

JOB *sleepily*
That Dame Fortune is one of those gypsies
Who leads us by the nose!
Who would like her backside
Chased after.

THE BURNING BUSH

Play 1911

To Käthe Richter
with love and gratitude

The Burning Bush

CHARACTERS

MAN
WOMAN
VIRGIN
MOTHER and BOY
MEN
WOMEN

SCENE ONE

The Woman's room, large French window with moonbeams shining in so that one can see out onto the roof.

WOMAN *in a white sheet, dressed for sleeping, such long hair that it trails on the floor behind her in ringlets. Ghostlike, she crawls out of the bedclothes and stands erect in the rays of light; the moon of electrical brightness.*

WOMAN   I dreamed a cart overheated — flung me up to heaven. There is nothing left to press my face down in my slumbers. To sleep I am too thirsty; a — drink!
she goes to the bell-pull — then forgets!
Where do the new rays come from? They drew me — waking me with all their strength. — I could no longer resist my feet. I am cold, can anyone see me?
louder
through the door
My shift and my skirt are not here, pass them in.
They are still asleep and I am awake.
sits in a chair, shivering with cold, her hair loose
The sterile heat of the unclear star is hanging all over me! Man in the moon — turn your back, don't look this way. Your radiant light gives strength to those who follow me on the stairs and come into my room.
Mr. Redveins gave me a slap across the face.
Mr. Darklooks wished me a very good day.
Mr. Loinpower plucked me a rose,
what do I care for the whole band of bedfellows.
downstairs the laughter of her drunken lovers can be heard. She washes her hands in the basin on the iron table, goes to the window, beckons
Come onto my bed, shadow, be my little darling creature — ugh — a cat, black as pepper, the breeze flung it in through my window.
opens the glass door and goes out onto the roof

The Burning Bush

Will he still come, will he come?
Time and again this apprehension in the whole of nature, from the roof right up to the sky. Everything waiting for a sigh of relief. My eyes cling to the sickle which shortens my close season.
By day I am a dubious being bearing a likeness to humanity. Tonight a man will breathe his breath into me and believe in the shape.
moonlight passing high above
O wondrous strange ways of men
that saw stars in circles
and light and shade into friendships braid.
O wonder-working ways of men
that made child-bearers out of ghosts.
Not long is my hour and already nigh! How brief is the time each thing has to blossom. The light of the moon is already about to fade. Unending pleasure. Soon I will no longer wish for anything. Not a cloud is left.
I abandon myself to the feverish wind, I am magnificently framed by my hair streaming out in rays, along the edge of my back, as regular as crests of water they run down my legs and disappear into the earth.

She sees someone creeping below, gives a start of fear and pleasure, beckons to him; a door suddenly bursts open, the Man glides silently in, a lighted candle in his hand.

WOMAN *before she sees him, singing*
All winter through an old man kept a bird.
When it was spring
it was too much for the bird,
so that it quite forgot to sing.
The old man spreads a green cloth over the iron bars of the birdcage;
still the bird has not merrily sung again to the old man.

WOMAN *to the Man* Did my singing bid you hearken?
Did you see my bars were open?

You imitate the cuckoo and fly to another's nest.
At the dead of night you see me!
How did you slip through wall and door?

MAN I guess, how could I know?
You have always been alone.
I was not with you. In the night your voice called the strangers and you meant me. And you truly hunger and greed for acts of love, and so I came up to you.

WOMAN Come, turn round toward me . . .
Why are you not good to me?
Clearly I dreamed you and in tears saw you only as day broke —
Was it wrong to beckon to you, as to so many others?
Now you are standing in the blissful radiance of the present.
My wish had the power to draw you to me in the darkness.
I am starving with love.
Only once I have given myself to you
shall I live through your pure strength alone.
. . . My arms draw yours — my legs make you walk.

Man comes closer, she gives a start

WOMAN You set my heart really pounding. My voice wants to be the sweetness of your mouth, my loins darken your blushing. — Do you feel sleepy all of a sudden?
Help! — my impotence is flowing into your strength. Alas!

The Man takes a sheet and wraps her up in it so that only her head is visible.

MAN *softly* Close your eyes,
and your wounds, too;
I have found you.

The Burning Bush

Man goes hesitantly to the exit, it grows dark, she takes her candlestick from the table in order to follow him, the open door blows out her light.

WOMAN Please — do not leave me behind, alone — my lord.
softly
As you vanish from my sight
Slowly I am seized by my plight.

MAN *reappearing in the doorway*
In the sky shines the morning star,
through the night, I wandered from afar!
Your faith called me to draw near!
I must not fear to be weaker,
as I was just now, here.

WOMAN *holding out a tentative hand to him*
Let your finger rest on mine,
give my faith in you this sign.
The question I wanted to ask,
Will you stay with me?
Will you go out from here
and leave your bride in temptation!
My breast is sick
like a flower in a lightless place.
Give me your hand once more, o loveless one.
Come, let me sit with you once more and close my eyes and sleep away all that has happened.
My lord — I am afraid; so weak am I, so strongly am I attached to you.

The Man kneels before the Woman and shines his light in her face, she lights her candle from his and regards him.

WOMAN Dearest, I have forgotten, I do not know where I was, you tell me.

MAN It is as if from my love
your own candle were lit,
now your body will feed it.
Tired of seeking who you are
you gave yourself to me.
Thus you came into being.
And if *I* now remove myself from you, like a veil, softly,
will you remain?
Let your soul awake, awake to birth.
And should the separation make you sad and drear,
mirrored in the night, my image will appear.
And once more your self-love's light
will be illumined by the tender image in the night.

The Man folds the sheet over her head — she wants to see him, he gently closes her eyes, in such a way that she sinks to her knees, he flees into the corridor.
The Woman, dazed, wakes up, follows him into the room where her drunken lovers are sleeping. The men wake up, the Woman looks through the barred window at the Man fleeing from her.

WOMAN *half asleep — half singing*
Sleepers, awake!
A white bird flew round the room, pecked out my eyes —
Sleepers, awake!
A red fish swam through, gorged itself on my blood —
Sleepers, break down the door!
A werewolf ran out, ate away my heart —

The young men throw their hats away — one is half naked, the girl gives him an encouraging look and runs after the crowd with him. They take sticks and pursue the fleeing Man — along a high stone embankment and up a ladder of iron rungs, fall — stop — the fleeing Man pauses to draw breath — turns, silhouetted against the sky, to meet his pursuers, grows weary — they surround him — beneath the railway bridge — a train passes — a bell sounds. The

fleeing Man takes the opportunity to drop from above into the water. They shoot, without hitting him.
Simultaneously with the Woman's last words a Salvation Army unit starts to sing the following, set to a hymn tune:

Who holds the key to love divine,
for him the hour will never fade.
How sweet will't be for him one day.
Earthly love is naught but pain,
a rose's thorn strewn on the way
to the garden gate of Golgotha Hill.
O my soul, stay not here still . . .

The last thing to be seen is the girl slipping away with the young man she gave the encouraging look.

SCENE TWO

A moonlit night. The room as before, Woman, hair loose, creeps to the window that is large and full of shadows, which change, covering the floor with shapes.

WOMAN *enticing, with a husky smile*
O — come to me in the night.
That you should be angry with me — I beg you,
because a stranger is lying with me in my bed.
Were it better not to be, than to be bad?
When being bad creates the semblance of being real?
I love you, the way you hate me.
The way I am, is the way you see.
weary, ill
No, I sleep in silent solitude,
my woman's hair my nightdress,
still stretched out on your hands.

And put my ear to the door,
And a bird was flying
— and hear you?
And put my eyes to the window
— And the moon was lying —
And embrace you?
restless
And the morning did not lie,
when I found myself alone and was a maid again.
Crying tears into my hair.
Pauses. Raises her arms in supplication again
A girl once whispered in your ear —
Honorably I gave myself to you —
Should not honor come from you to me in return?
dreaming, musing
What I lost, *myself*, shall I find again in you?
What is darker than the night in which I gave birth to new longings alone!
What is whiter than the night in which I hope to bear miracles?
And what is redemption and deliverance,
Why for women are the right men sweet
and do women yearn for the stranger.
The right man knew —
the stranger tempted.
Woe to my body!
cries out again in a fearful questioning. Both rooms can be seen

MAN *in the other room, singing in an unnatural voice, without moving, whitish light, door open, which now throws in light, rays of light from the two rooms cross and seek each other at mid-height*
The deep-as-water was sleeping,
The mountain stood shadow-bare
And time was not
And there was no beast to hear
And there was no fire to warm

96 The Burning Bush

Nor to burn any flames,
When love was not.
And then . . .
rays of light rise up and play and meet again , coming to rest
Water roared after water,
And mountain darkened mountain.
Time tugged —
And beasts smote humans and ate them
and spewed them forth.
And flames open up red wounds,
Where love turned sweet to man and woman.

The Man is lying on the bed, rigid, not taking his eye off the Woman. Lights slowly dim in the Woman's room, her breathing is scarcely audible and becoming weak. She speaks the following in a terribly sad, full and warm voice.

WOMAN *staggering to the door* Of love my parents ate; from that I became a human.
O thou human! Who knew me.
Help! . . . Falling! . . .

She falls down

MAN May hope make you rise. Soon you will go out of the house. As you rush around, the dim lamp will melt away which gives the pain to such distress, life to the flickering. The bride will see the bolt open in her chamber. Already the life-color grows pale! Wing-beats, that are you yourself, blow at the wick.
The fire asks, where shall I put myself!
And dies down in the ashes.

Strange enough and unmiserable . . .

WOMAN . . . the light of day closes over me.

SCENE THREE

In the forest, Woman in her shift, face looking ill, unconsciously looking for a particular direction, white ground, tree-trunks black, sky black, no light apart from the reflection of the white ground; Men and Women.

WOMAN *moaning like a woman about to give birth*
Woe is me —
he is living with my strength.
Somewhere.
Woe is me —
I am weak.
When he was with me and I touched his hem, in a fever —
I shrank back from him.
You are leading me astray! Where?
angrily, screaming, gradually getting higher
Then, all at once, he was imbued with fire and suffused with light,
and my warm blood leapt up within me,
I was cold and my teeth were chattering.
writhing in horror
Away from here —
Ill-starred bed . . .
Unresting place!
Sacrificial stall.

OLD MAN *takes her for a sick liar*
Seeking his trail,
round and round we go,
Flickering, moonbright flames aglow.
With lanterns shining through the haze,
We cast light through the forest.
A wary vulture voids in its nest.

WOMAN *ecstatic* Everywhere a human voice — you —
Somewhere I hear your call —

A SECOND OLD MAN We seek the man
who abandoned a woman.
A hunting beast cried out.

They strike against the trees to rout him out.

WOMAN See, he snarls at me from the thorns!
He wakes up at the shouting!
Look at him!
— Like water-thunder, roaring ever louder —
All-embracing embrace!!
The human face —
You in a dream — your sweet smell . . .
Your fire-red head smothered in the cloak of the sun?

A THIRD MAN *softly* A flash of lightning quivered and burned the tame herd to ashes.

WOMAN A flood you are, your hearing all around me . . .
Woe!
He broke in.
He is grazing inside me.

FIRST WOMAN Listen to what she is saying;
The morning warmth is rising,
Light-clear, the sunstar pierces the haze.
Nature disorients her —

WOMAN Go, go with soft steps
so that none will scare his nearness away.
How much good comes to me from you!
I send, I send my bridal wishes to you!
screaming
My eye goes dim —
Have I died?
As I feel his miracle,

A graveyard will be my wedding-bed and weeping my wedding-cry.

Collapses in the middle of the stage and lies there, motionless, like a bundle of clothes.

SECOND WOMAN The angel guides her,
tear-soaked hair covers her eyes
and she sees him?
Her mind is disturbed.
May an angel guide her.
restless

THIRD WOMAN Which way to turn?
Three paths are open,
Each take one.

Three men from the chorus, each, separate from the others, follows one path; in front of them three pictures open up. Each describes what he sees, slowly getting louder, each only lit as long as he is speaking.

FIRST OLD MAN I see a man on the ground grieving.
His beard soiled in the dust.
His heart beating loud.
He thirsts because you offered him
the sponge soaked in vinegar.

SECOND OLD MAN I see him indistinctly!
With you he took the body out of a chalice — and you blasphemed.
I see again —
A call! Lost travelers?
A yearning heart.
Is it he?

THIRD MAN I see a metal man locked to an animal in heat. And did you see, then, that the animal was eating his heart. He stirs.

The Burning Bush

The chain stretched round him clatters in two.
His glittering hand is victorious in the doubting combat.
His metal call awakes the woman emerging from the animal's skin.
Woman, who treads the serpent underfoot,
your heart is swelling with mother-joy.

A radiant light. Restless clamor, men and women reach out for open hands, call out, sob, for a moment one can see many open hands.

CHORUS *men to women, agitated, loud and soft*
I see you now with a different eye,
You are no longer a stranger to me!
I forgot you and see you with love once more.
Your body has grown meaningful.
What happened, that I spent years living alongside you!
And however often you opened your heart — I was not worthy to enter into you.
What is this I feel . . .
Now I pay heed, silent tidings and strange comprehension reach me.
Fearful lips.
Lost words come.
An alien world, joy, bliss.

It slowly grows dark

CHORUS *going off chanting toward the backcloth*
I believe in the resurrection within me
I believe in the resurrection within me —
I believe in the resurrection within me —.

It grows quite dark. The clamor of voices can still be heard during this scene, later growing weaker and less clear; empty space. Light slowly falls from above onto the center of the stage, now one can see a girl on the spot where the Woman was lying. She is lying on the ground, ecstatic, talking softly to herself, full of suppressed rejoicing. Thin voice — swelling like birdsong.

VIRGIN Out of the valley the lark is flying to its heavenly home. I would like to put my arms unseen around my lover, like a bush round the new rose.
I am so happy since he descended on me.
Why are not all people good?

SCENE FOUR

Man and Woman opposite one another on two rocky ledges, the chorus indistinctly visible in the dark of the background, Man warding off, Woman grandiose. Undulating, palm-like grasses and clumps of fern. As long as he is speaking, white light, alternating with red as soon as she answers.

WOMAN This whiteness casts a spell.
My body is a burning, fiery bush,
O you my man! Nourishing wind!
My breasts two tongues of fire,
O you, unwilling voice!
My hands hot wings,
my legs burning coals —
white and red — white-hot, red-hot;
in the fiery cloak of long torment, hot with shame,
I burn, and yet am not consumed.
Enter in to me, put out the fire and redeem me.

MAN Woman in childbed, hopelessly laboring!
Who, for weakness, does not dare to give birth!
Have for that no better time in mind —
so that after, gently shivering,
you can lie down to rest!
Let us later soothe the pain,

when one of us, tired, is
rolled in the linen.
Already fanned into flame is that which would
become a light,
unlike smoking fire, which brings tears to the eye.
Fire burns to ashes,
Light at the last has a kindly look!

WOMAN *startled*
Figure of death!
You duped me! I thought you were flesh, blood!
You gathered within me, a raging flood!
Sun bleaches the moon —
Freezing frost
Pierces my flesh.
Pierces my flesh.
Around me the man who wrestled with me,
who pushed down every thought,
knocked them down . . .
Will not leave
my blood and bone —
mocking
Rapacious beast who sucked me dry!
The peace you bring hurts, tears me to pieces.
I cannot greet you, dear man,
who me as sacrifice rejected
in the mute interval of fear!
O take me from this world of torture.

MAN Truly are you human? With your long hair!

WOMAN Why are you not good —
O Man who overran me with desires.
I know you would be
both lover and liberator
to me, the unclean, unknown —

Yet are my deadly foe,
My dungeoner!

She gives a start — weeping.

MAN My love-force, outpoured, everywhere sucked up by you,
in peaks alone — softly darkening, softly transfiguring —
does it touch you, otherness, self-willed, phantom other-self?
Woman is innocent.
But man — in his thorns the frost of restlessness grows lone.
At times within you, quietly, as if dreaming on.
Eyes drained of tears, turning round
in farewell glance, you look me in the face . . .
Maternal chamber, open up!
Heavenly home, draw your errant son.
Weary I am.
Woman, go free out of my hands.

WOMAN *throwing the stone that hits him on the chest*
I no longer acknowledge you.

MAN Have pity!
You hurt me,
you, by whom I am unloosed.
Ah, see here my life
float away in the blood of sacrifice.
The earth can scarce accept the force,
which from me issued, from me poured.
You leave me to my ruin,
brought on by you whom I set free.
In mortal anguish, who can comfort me?
Sister, dry my brow.

WOMAN *falls onto him and pushes the others back. With great love*
Leave me.
My man is to be untouched!

I suffer with you!
Go not yet, go not in haste from me.
See now I am coming to you.

MAN Believe me, and your hand in blessing inflicts a closing wound on me — Why are we not good!

SCENE FIVE

Room in which Man, lying on the bed with an open wound, is dying. Woman bending over him. Grouped together as in a Pietà. — Mother and Boy pass through. Boy adolescent.

BOY Tell me, what is the woman staring at so fixedly? And tell me softly in my ear Mother, those who suffer so, are they full of sins?
becoming aroused
Mother, are you a woman?
What you are throws me into confusion!
I am suffering with the beautiful woman, I want to go to her.

MOTHER O sore mother's death and foreboding childish wonder.
Not for the world! Go not, look not on them,
When they are paying with blood and cannot unite.

BOY Give peace to those who live here!
A grave-mound full of mourner-folk.
I stand at the gate.
God puts his head in his hand and cries.

MOTHER I can see it otherwise!
A thornbush suddenly burned.
The drought creeps off like a worm.
God lets the light rise up to him.
departing

CHORUS *standing by the wall; dressed in mourning*
In her heart his image is with glowing charcoal sketched.
Does she shine on him?

Does he still live?

I put an apple in his hand and the fruit has already turned quite brown.

He has closed his eyes to the invisible.
I know the dying are good, they take mortal pain.

In the meantime the light has formed a glory over the main group. The sun goes down.
Nimbus — Woman and Man speak in their sleep, in high, unnatural voices, in such a way that each sound is gripping.

MAN Am I alive — **You and I.**

WOMAN Lost,
forgotten years
wash over me, seep away.
Burnt white.

MAN Time was horrifying.
Gauntlet of desire — sacrificial beast!
softly dying
And to fall into oblivion!

WOMAN Silently a vision dissolves.

Man dead. The humming stops for a moment. A glory of light has been formed, all raise their hands, give signs.

CHORUS *separates into two groups; half singing, half speaking*
And thus died a human who has understood himself.

106 *The Burning Bush*

MEN OF THE CHORUS You are my silent gazing.

WOMEN OF THE CHORUS *going up to the bed alternately with the men*
You are my shuddering,
you are my light,
suffused with radiance,
and I enter in concealed
and you are made manifest to me.
But I lost myself
— and I remembered . . .

CHORUS *of the men*
Oblivion: calling without sound.
Oblivion: to **be**, once, and once alone.
Oblivion: earthly bliss.

WOMEN Oblivion: flowing blood without healing.
Oblivion: teeth quivering in starving desire.

CHORUS *question*
Why are you not good?
Why are you not good?

CHORUS *answer*
Because their ought was **being**
but their want mere seeming.

WHOLE CHORUS Forced forth, there appears a vision,
a world to consciousness.
And once more, from the image to which it clings,
the creation looses itself.
The void takes on the form of water, air and earth.
Fire burns it for ever and fire consumed it.

ORPHEUS AND EURYDICE

Play, 1918

Orpheus and Eurydice

CHARACTERS

HADES
CUPID
ORPHEUS
EURYDICE
PSYCHE
FIRST FURY
SECOND FURY
THIRD FURY
WARRIORS
COUNTRY FOLK
SAILORS
WOMEN
THE DEAD

TIME
The past

PLACE
First act: garden and house of Orpheus
Second act: the Underworld, on the way to the sea, a bark
Third act: back in Orpheus' native land

ACT ONE

SCENE ONE

Eurydice is sitting on the terrace of her garden. She is looking across to the mountains. On the floor a basket with sewing things. Eurydice is wrapped in an undyed lamb's fleece, under which she has a flowing, violet robe; her hair tumbles down in blond ringlets. On one finger Eurydice is wearing a ring with the portrait of Orpheus; she is reading the inscription. A carriage arrives; the horses' bells can be heard. Orpheus comes in from the street. He is blinded by the change from the bright light to the shady arbor with its luxuriant foliage. He clutches at thin air and knocks the sewing basket over with his foot; a child's ball rolls out. Eurydice gives a soft laugh. Orpheus throws the ball into Eurydice's lap, kisses her on the forehead, gently pushing her head backward as he does so.

EURYDICE
You're back?
almost reproachfully
So soon?

ORPHEUS
And you, — as if not alone?
As if you were thinking something through —

EURYDICE
As this ring welds together Orpheus and Eurydice, so shall
turns the ring
the one ever find happiness in the other. That was it.
pouting
I watched you this morning
as you drove past in your carriage
without waving.
How could you!
Thinking of nothing but yourself, your own happiness?

aside
No! I cannot act out this part, cannot be cool toward him!
aloud
My long-awaited love!
Your head, as you drove past, leaned back,
For greeting I took it.
Your eyes, like two birds, flew straight to me.
O fair sight!
Could I never look my fill —
Does not the rime of bitterness melt in a double sun!
From her husband she who sits here his being takes and watches o'er it.
Now I have it, and this, out there, perplex'd me:
The carriage ever smaller grew, at last a dot,
containing your face, which, for me, became — no smaller!
Through the distorted glass of the world I saw your turn-out alone;
oh, it glided past! —
The wheels, vying in diminution, and bearing my being away from me,
you, full possession, did not carry off with them,
nor diminish.
Orpheus! Could I ever forget you?
In the half-open door Psyche appears, adolescent, mischievous, carrying a small snake in her arm

EURYDICE
It's you, my child?
Come on in.

PSYCHE *shy with Orpheus, restless eyes, flushed*

EURYDICE
What does that look mean?

PSYCHE *mysteriously*
Sister! Why is a door like a riddle?

EURYDICE *giving the door a bewildered glance, then laughing, trying to go along with the joke*

PSYCHE *like a teacher explaining to a child*
There's something in both that — was nothing before.
That's what happens if people are curious!

EURYDICE *clapping her hands*
Tell me, who was it taught you that?

PSYCHE *throwing her arms round Eurydice's neck*
I dreamed it. —

EURYDICE
Off you go now.

PSYCHE
Not to bed, it's still light.
— I was going out to play with my dream,
suddenly three strange women were standing there,
and then the three women asked me
who my father is —

EURYDICE *softly to Orpheus*
You must guard it.
Some things she knows, and conceals what she lives for.
All her whims are often tests.
That just now was an example.
You must talk to her of her father
so that she does not look behind her.

ORPHEUS *to Psyche, hesitantly, earnestly*
The one who has no body, yet has the power to move us,
released you, spirit, for a while from the free air,
here to serve Eurydice. —
Your father!

Should his violent power break her, you are to be of use to her —
for good; you, in form like her, companion to her, the
lightning bolts must temper, and the onslaught of fate, that weaves its
web through you, must backward steer.
at the balustrade, speaking out into the open air, in a different tone
Today, after the rain, a new star emerged.

EURYDICE
Psyche knows all the stars.
*the star flickers in the evening light. Psyche's dress flutters, as if
she herself were about to float away. Eurydice takes her arm*

PSYCHE *an ecstatic cry*
Eurydice, let go of me!
There is the star flying in the sky!
Now it is falling —
leaves softly, then starts running in the garden

EURYDICE
Where has Psyche gone? Turn back, child!
You were almost too happy.
If the stars to the gazing soul shine not
from far beyond earthly confines,
oh, then is our pale spring dream —
realized. And the, and the time of waiting over —

ORPHEUS
Tears in her innermost being? For these first, innocent ones
pain has no salt as yet —
*Eurydice brings the child back, stroking her hair back from her
brow*

EURYDICE
I blow away the dust of the fields and see
my little face, that came back home so late today.
holding the snake, Psyche falls asleep in Eurydice's arms

ORPHEUS
Let me kneel at your feet, suffer
you to soothe me, as you did this angel
— or beckon ghosts!
Oh, such grace! My madness!
No, let me speak — I love you,
love you more than happiness!

EURYDICE
I wonder if joys, even with wings, can extend over life?
How her little face twitches!

ORPHEUS *over Psyche's forehead, draws the oval of Eurydice's face*
Does not the shadow of this innocently sleeping child cover your face,
that is so close to me;
And do not the features, so familiar to me I could draw
every detail from memory, arouse the desire for likening?
Your brow, your chin, the ray from the cloud of your eyes,
if I could hold all that, more, once again?

EURYDICE
Were she our child!
I am all the joy that came to you!
Happiness — that you must hold fast!
aside
I can never wholly pass away, once a life rests here,
put forth from uncertain darkness,
born of our loving urge
— like light, love ever passes on its spark.
pulling apart the edges of her dress over her breast, Eurydice places Orpheus' hand on her heart
"My happiness is her heart, now I hold it."
Do you agree?

ORPHEUS
One, and one — when I count the pulses,

my own beats steal into yours.
One, two! Orpheus, my sweet, is sighing out his life!

EURYDICE
You let your imagination run wild, love —

ORPHEUS
Love is so insane. "Die! Die!" it lures us on.
Laughing in its game of hide-and-seek love would think up this place!
Here my lyre will beat; behind the lilac Orpheus will see Eurydice's face!

EURYDICE
May it be long yet before happiness, losing its thousand forms,
in a cloud forsakes you and your lust for life.

ORPHEUS
Whatever lusting need has found to slake its thirst,
as a slave it is fettered to it;
But what is more unfettered, goddess, more inventive than love?

EURYDICE
If you see me smile, it's at the goddess,
whom a centaur fell in love with;
and forced an embrace — from her cloud-shape.

ORPHEUS
How he rears up, his brow kissed by the intoxication
of being! Triumph of happiness, to live life to the full!

EURYDICE
How she dissolves into air, glowing with abandon —
love! — Without a beloved! — Only desire!
Kiss me without end! Close up my mouth!

Orpheus and Eurydice 115

ORPHEUS
With breath like a puff of hoar-frost —

EURYDICE
I cannot tell, is this still me escaping? —
death of feeling —

ORPHEUS
Happiness! Every word Eurydice spoke
carves a memory for me,
how every breath unleashes storms in the heart, where Orpheus, sun flashes!

EURYDICE
Unhappiness — is it bathed in gold? False — is happiness too?
False this joy? — For the centaur died in the fire!

ORPHEUS
Seek-sorrows foresee unhappiness, happiness is not false!

EURYDICE
Have I not a duty to be honest with my lord;
like the centaur, happiness I feel in your heat,
one day, to dissolve into a handful of ashes? —
in the woods a frightened calf calls for its mother

EURYDICE *half carrying the child, half dragging it into the chamber*
How content that mother will be, who is now suckling her babe.

SCENE TWO

Psyche sleeping outside a door leading to Eurydice's chamber. She hears everything in her sleep. Knocking outside

PSYCHE
Something evil is crouching on the threshold.
louder
Who are you? Be off with you!

THE THREE FURIES *invisible. A torch waving from side to side; softly*
With a commission from Hades.

FIRST FURY *interrupts*
With a request,
won't you open the door?

ALL THREE *continuing*
This is where Eurydice lives?

PSYCHE *frightened, louder*
I'm not telling! Whether she lives here or not. —
Quick, Cupid, my little dove, quick!
Get rid of that torch!
In a little while Cupid will
slip through the veil of twilight
and with invisible fingers
unloosen Psyche's locks.
Take the light away!
He might think morning had come and disappear.

SECOND FURY *in a low voice*
Psyche needs dark nights to spin her web,
so her feathered archer will fly into it!

THIRD FURY *to the second Fury, angrily*
Do you have to open your big mouth so wide, you silly goose!

SECOND FURY *to third Fury*
If you would shut yours first!

FIRST FURY *aside*
I'll get Cupid for myself!
Just like a cat snatching a dove.
If it's night, and dark, I'll prattle like Psyche.
to Psyche
Sister, you can tell me, what makes you so sad?
What night brought becomes uncertain with each new day?
You should watch the gate better before Cupid disappears.
I'd be happy to stand guard.

PSYCHE *restless*
What should I do? I will — not see him — not while I'm sleeping,
ever. — Only feeling his embrace, never allowed to ask.
If only I could look at him, for one whole day, hold him
without letting him free himself from the tender shackle.

THIRD FURY
A vicious monster with bat's wings he is by day, your nightmare!
To warm himself up, every night he lies on your heart!
Your man in the moon, ha! a dead man!

PSYCHE *starts in her sleep, throws her hands around, then calms down*
Just leave at once, you and your quarrels!

SECOND FURY
That silly girl will smash my nose in!
Do you mind, it's fragile as porcelain!
How can we get round her — I'm on pins and needles.

THIRD FURY
It's driving me mad!

FIRST FURY *slyly*
Hm. — The little lambkin will escape the young whippersnapper yet.
Listen!
to Psyche
Miss Psyche!
I'd like to enter your service as chambermaid.
I'll just pop the torch in through the door.
I'll cover it right away. Open up.

PSYCHE
And then?

FIRST FURY
Why, while you and Cupid are dallying in close embrace,
by the light of the torch I'll have a quick look, so I can
tell you in the morning how fair he is.
Thus, when the poor light of day breaks,
you can still dream of the sweet vision of the night.

PSYCHE *crying in her sleep*
Tell me, my tears, was it a sin merely to listen?

FIRST FURY
Psyche is weeping as sleepy children weep.
If a speck of sin gets in your eye, quickly you wash it out
with the salt water.

SECOND FURY *to the third, softly*
Kind words are soothing milk, only the cheese
they make stings.
Come on! We must not suffer this insolence any longer!
To Eurydice we go.

PSYCHE *joyfully*
There he comes!
I beg you, put your torch out —

FIRST FURY
Don't leave us sitting out here in the vestibule,
let us in by the door.
By the light of the torch!
Otherwise the bird will have flown.

PSYCHE *still asleep, opens the door leading to Eurydice; three shadows, now visible, push in through the door; half waking up, she stands in front of the door, trying to keep the Furies out*
To hell! To hell! To hell!

ALL FURIES *waving the torch, mimicking her*
To heaven! To heaven! To heaven!
with insolent laughter
We're staying till Cupid comes.
Us? Go?
The very idea! Has the penny dropped now?
The Furies never back off.

FIRST FURY *beside the door; covers the torch, at which Psyche goes back to sleep*
I'll take you back to bed.

PSYCHE *enraptured, while the shadows slip in through the door*
There he is, drawn by his team of doves!
the Third Fury sees Cupid coming and shines the light on him behind Psyche's back

PSYCHE
The doves shy?
Their wings droop, sore?
His airy chariot, overturning —

borne along by bright blue eyes, splintering?
Cupid falling out! Oh! he covers his face with his
hands — Cupid, I — no, you — I'm trembling,
as if I had — committed the greatest wrong!
Because I — what? — wanted a peek at my
happiness, my jealousy blocked your flight.
Cupid blind?
Halt, Fury, you have betrayed me!
Your evil eye came racing along — blind?

FIRST FURY
Take note! How you love Cupid!

PSYCHE
Alas! Awake! Eurydice! The Furies!

SCENE THREE

the three Furies in the doorway of Eurydice's chamber

ALL THREE FURIES *solemnly*
Our mission, you must descend to Hades
and bring unhappiness upon Orpheus.

EURYDICE *shattered*
Importunates! Withdraw outside the wall!
Let me embrace him.

THIRD FURY *continuing their message*
For seven years you must forget him.

EURYDICE
Dead for seven years?
One thing is true: I refuse to leave him!

Orpheus and Eurydice 121

FURIES *grab her clothes, try to pull her to the door*

EURYDICE
I cannot, paralyzed, move my foot from the spot.
Without seeing him? Orpheus!

FURIES *to each other*
It is not up to us to compel her to leave. What to do?

FIRST FURY *to Eurydice*
Then we must spend the night here and talk to him.
We will persuade him, there will be no lack of opportunity, we have come to visit you, to take you out for a day. Then he will come in time and aid our intent.

EURYDICE
Importunates, withdraw outside the walls!
Let me only, out of your sight, embrace him.
One more night.

FIRST FURY
Would you have the heart to add even more to his bitterness?

EURYDICE
Hypocrite! Let me have him, without your lie, one more night.
Before I must go from him.

THREE FURIES *softly*
Then make good use of your night.
crouching at the back
Orpheus has heard the last exchange; at Eurydice's cry he had come, unobserved by her, into the chamber

ORPHEUS *to Eurydice, who has a tender conscience*
You are leaving me?

EURYDICE
To belong to you!

ORPHEUS
Because you intend to go away?
Can you lie to me?

THREE FURIES *clasping Eurydice; in a firm, soft tone*
She comes with us today.
For that we came this night, to ask for her from you.

EURYDICE
To Hades' land. That is all.

ORPHEUS
Flee from me? To the land of shades?

EURYDICE *gently and firmly*
That is where my journey takes me —

FIRST FURY *evasively*
Who would want to journey there?

ORPHEUS *to Eurydice*
It is a long way to Death. A whole life away!
suspiciously
I do not know your whole mind on this!
Eurydice! You, who are alive like me!
to the Furies
She does not tell your lie very well. All this is
to Eurydice
a delusion. And you will not go from me?
These vultures are hovering round our bliss.

EURYDICE
O beloved! Even in a thousand deaths I love you even more!

The three Furies prepare a meal on the table at the back and bring a white shroud, in which they clothe Eurydice

ORPHEUS
Why this dress?

EURYDICE
I know this night is drawing to a close, so I have dressed myself.
swaying
The ground is swaying beneath me —
smiling at Orpheus in the effort to control herself
All I want from you is steadfastness.
looking at the ground, pale

ORPHEUS
Is that a vision arising from the abyss?
Your gaze so drawn to the depths, so fixed on them!
You see my open arms near, and do not
dare to trust yourself to them!

EURYDICE *takes Orpheus by the hand and leads him to the table*
Why should one who may stay alive thirst after reasons
that do not impel him!
That's why I go. Follow me.
shakes her head, laughs

ORPHEUS
Tears and laughter scud across your face.
Eurydice sits down at the table with Orpheus, puts food in front of him; neither touch the food. Both grow sad; shades crouch in the background. The snake drinks out of the bowl of milk Eurydice has set on the floor for it

ORPHEUS
Then will I be merry with you, as far as I am able.

Orpheus and Eurydice

Eurydice forces herself to be cheerful, drinks to Orpheus out of his glass

EURYDICE
Tell me, are you content with me now?
The wine that was in the cup is drunk. Drink no more,
my heart, just now.
If you did, who knows what you would find in the cup —
the Furies slowly stand up; in horror, Orpheus and Eurydice grasp each other's hand, the ring slips off Eurydice's hand and falls to the ground, the snake bites Eurydice's heel

ORPHEUS
Why do I feel as if I were drunk with happiness?

EURYDICE
Now we see all too well that in like thoughts
we came together. Unhappiness remained in my hand.
Take you this — unhappiness, my gift to you.
falls dead into the arms of the Furies, who clasp her and carry her from the chamber

THE THREE FURIES
The snake has drunk its milk, now it will sleep.
Let us go, we thank you for
your hospitality.

ACT TWO

SCENE ONE

three years later, in the Underworld. Psyche sees Eurydice among the shades

VOICE OF EURYDICE, *from within the Underworld*
What harmonies — what hope —

PSYCHE *directing her voice toward Eurydice*
If of Orpheus quickly I speak,
will you listen? Eurydice!

EURYDICE *voice*
Who is Orpheus?
Orpheus is without form, is like this island.
Are you the melodious sound of human tongue
that you move me so?

PSYCHE
Psyche must serve you —
to outwit Hades I advised Orpheus, dragged down here
by longing while he still draws breath,
to descend into the Underworld.

ORPHEUS *from the entrance to the Underworld*
How you have thrown, greedy Orcus, your shadow
over the whole life of all those whom you receive.
Now too over me!
So no, not even one final moment in pain any more?
After, as so often, egotism plumbed it to the very depths.
One limb, one trait of mine telltale still?
No flinching before the final deal!
Eurydice! Orpheus is unto death bereft of hope.
Do you hear?

Orpheus and Eurydice

Down to the cold ones in vain I seek a path.
Open your eyes, since mine are dim and wet.
Dry are yours like the ashes here?
Has Psyche already brought you the news?
Free Eurydice for one short summer, take my life in exchange!
Give me your hand on it, Hades:
For Eurydice — my skin as ransom!
Orpheus, making his way through the moldy fog, tries to find Eurydice among the shades, going from group to group. Some try to lick his hand, while others grab those who are kneeling by their hands and feet and, gloating, thrust them into a pit. Beggars on crutches are spreading garbage from sacks around which lazy fat shades gather to eat and argue; madmen try to climb up the walls and slide down. Murderers with daggers pounce on Orpheus' shadow. Lovers crawl off on all fours when he approaches, clustering together like a swarm. Some have animal faces, or tails and claws. Giggling, muttering, shrill laughter from within.
Eurydice, in an ecstatic trance, like an angel in this wretched place, dressed in white, wrapped according to the burial custom in a long veil, the ends of which drag along the ground, is guided by Psyche. At her appearance and meeting with Orpheus, all pause in their senseless activities and listen

PSYCHE *hurrying on ahead of Eurydice toward Orpheus, who is in the center of the stage. Softly, hurriedly*
Orpheus, turn away!
If you fix not your eyes upon her,
alarm her not with images of the past,
consciousness, that has deserted Eurydice, will return.

EURYDICE *fainting, tries to cry out*
Pull away the veil — Psyche, what is happening?
staggers and touches him
Orpheus! Here, Orpheus, — this is my hand —
Orpheus is deeply moved, but, following Psyche's advice, looks away. Eurydice falls to her knees

EURYDICE
Ah, forgive me, forgive me the long years!
Orpheus, face turned aside, carries her to the way out into the world. All the shades wring their hands

EURYDICE
Forgotten, Orpheus? Never more!

ORPHEUS
Forgotten? Eurydice, never!

PSYCHE *left by herself*
Forgotten, Psyche is left behind.
the mists close behind the two as they climb up out of the Underworld

SCENE TWO

The path out of the crater, the exit from the Underworld: beneath cascades of mist, over manifold fissures in the lava which, covered in ice, run along the edge of the path but which more and more recede, so that the view opens out, through snow-covered slopes, onto a pleasant sea shore below. Thaw. Fir branches drop piles of snow onto the thawing path; the lower down it gets, the warmer the day becomes. Eurydice emerges from the ice, like a burden on Orpheus' arm. A flight of doves through a gap in the mist that reveals the sea.

ORPHEUS
Floating beings, released from a fist!
The upward gaze plunges, turns inward.
Image of space impatient to appear in small compass.
Sending wishful creations soaring,
which, like calm in our breast, our mood long ignored.

Orpheus and Eurydice

EURYDICE
One downy feather raises the warmth!
more lively
— I take it as a sign.
Just so it was when you, Orpheus,
for the first time whispered Eurydice's name.
I found a new lease of life and, to please you,
climbed the path out into the world.
Feel my strength!
A marvel how a woman's heart can strengthen
if you beat your heartbeat in time!
How light my step and free of sorrow!
Is it not the former happy being holding you in heartfelt nearness?
See how light my foot is.

ORPHEUS
Give me your arm more firmly.

EURYDICE
With one glance you sought the ring on my finger?

ORPHEUS
So far affection has kept its power to soothe —

EURYDICE *suspicious, then cheerful once more*
— but still, when you explain things to yourself?
So you think.
Keep going, Orpheus. Follow me.
No brooding.
To judge the sweet, doubly sweetened drink
by the last drop in the cup,
the lees can easily taste bitter.

ORPHEUS
I have reached the point, I would have thought —
Wait —

EURYDICE *stumbles, falls laughing into Orpheus' arm*
— here I am tumbling like a raging current down to the sea,
reeling and clinging onto your neck, Orpheus.

ORPHEUS
Instead of you in my arm, for years fear
was entwined with hope.
The chain drags along behind me.
Although I was not tempted
to cling onto past sorrows, vexations,
equally barren gifts from hell.
As some to thorns, stones, in their fall.
Eurydice, dip your hand in the light —
A sail down there does not deceive us?
pointing to the sea. The sails of a black bark are to be seen standing out against the water in the mist and light. Eurydice gives a start when she sees the bark
Look! Mirroring the far horizon, joy again depths will know!
Come, fresher air will color your cheeks
once we put out to sea.

EURYDICE *aside*
To sea in Hades' craft? — I?
— Is that what you whisper?
I no longer know what was mine.
Irresolute, Eurydice stands on the jetty behind Orpheus. Orpheus pushes her in front of him

ORPHEUS
Sailing off, you can look round from your flight.
Brooding along the way offers little prospect for us.
Look ahead, docked at a jetty.
You go in front.
I want to see, in the sail's joyous progress
away from an irksome yesterday,
you on the immeasurable expanse

writing my trail.

EURYDICE *hesitating*
Does heartbeat confuse? I and thou. —
And something more? Fear of you?
pleading
Lies and deceit — Orpheus — you go —

ORPHEUS
The middle of the day is opening up for us both
to pass through.
Nothing can force its way between us.
Like a spider whose prey gave it the slip
the night writhes beneath us and takes itself off.
Do you feel safe? And I? — We alone —

EURYDICE
May it remain so. It is not yet too late.

ORPHEUS
Too late to go back, my love. Let us haste.
Who knows how long all this will stay within grasp.

EURYDICE
— The hope that day will break again tomorrow!
Little flowers! How clearly do I feel
your fetters loosening.
The spring — like green velvet! —
Pressing its face against the bars. —
I want no memory of former days.

ORPHEUS *lifting her on board*
The sails will speed us away.

EURYDICE
The warmth lifts one downy feather,

Say it — one word — I live.
Your head bows. Do not try to guess
Why Eurydice is silent.
Oh, what I did, you came upon it.
Be kind, pick it up and give it back to me.
the gangway is raised, the boat departs

SCENE THREE

On the bark. Dead calm. Constellations with a black cloud below them. At the front of the stage is the cabin, which is curtained off with a mat hanging in front of it (until the middle of the fourth scene). The three Furies are squatting on the deck, weaving a net, occasionally raising the curtain slightly and peeping into the cabin. The foolish sailor, the moonlight shining on him, falls asleep at the helm; tormented by the blazing heat he rolls across the stage to the ship's railing, close to the Furies, and stares down at the sea, at the glowing image of the moon

ALL SAILORS *as they fall asleep on the upper deck*
Cupid!
We clasp our hands and ask
for wind, a favorable wind.
We would like to fly like your
doves!
Bring us safe to the green land.

FIRST FURY
to the second
Instead of gawking at the simple-minded
lad, turning at the grill
so he gets some of the heat
in which the chestnuts are roasting,
keep close to the wall,
keep an eye on Eurydice,

instead of gawking the other way.

THIRD FURY
Would not the simpleton be good
at pulling chestnuts out of the fire
for us? I fear it will come to blows?

FIRST FURY
Be quiet and wet your finger
instead of your tongue, to weave
the net, mesh by mesh,
Eurydice's misfortune.

THIRD FURY
Three more knots to go.
This one will hold!
There goes the next one through my teeth.
Just one more bite.
Why did Hades let that little chick
escape with Orpheus; I'd like
to get my teeth into her!

FIRST FURY
Only to fatten it up!
Hades had to take the rogue
in the poke as well;
without the cock the chick won't eat!
I had a good look at him, that down-and-out Orpheus!
Put a ring on a lead round his
leg to keep track of him.
We're not to go behind his back.
It's an honest deal with Hades!

SECOND FURY *listening*
I think Orpheus is going behind
his own back. He truly has a task

that now makes him laugh, now
angry!
That has so absorbed him for seven years
he has not seen the sun come up
or go down.

FIRST FURY *to the Fool*
Boy! You! Believe me —
to the other Furies
Any minute the throwaway game
with the numskull can start
to the Fool
— if you lean over, numskull,
along with your poise you'll lose your avoirdupois,
nothing will pull you down, you will fly!
Want to bet? Here, I'll wager my head!

THE FOOL
Believe you?
Aren't those maggots growing out of your
death's head, bats, wing-fish,
dusty hawkmoths?
Ugh! It would make my flesh crawl!

THIRD FURY
Larvae that sprout wings
fly away as summer flies.
It's we old women, boy,
who are left empty-handed!

THE FOOL
Suddenly a gentle breeze
so cool around my brow —

THIRD FURY
What can you see on the bottom?

THE FOOL
A fishwife, alone there, swaying,
as if consumed by torrid blue,
now cooled by azure green, with
swelling fins, waving —

THIRD FURY
Wouldn't you, o man, like to
go under in the water?

THE FOOL
A pebble first, to see how deep.
Splash!
But it sets off in my breast an
unpleasant echo —

THIRD FURY
Don't you long to take the fishwife in your arms?
In the water, the darling —
In the ship scarce one nail sits firm.
Can't you hear the planks
in its ribcage creaking?

THE FOOL *runs off, shouting*
A leak!
A leak!
the sailors hear it in their sleep, repeat it

ALL SAILORS
A leak!
A leak!
Bail out the water! — quick, make a chain with the pail!
Take it easy — easy —
Plug in the bung —
they calm down again; the Fool recovers his nerve and returns to the Furies

THIRD FURY
If the boy is so timid, he'll never be father to a man!
Look down again, what do you see?
Use your brain —

THE FOOL
If you look down along
your legs, both standing together,
in harmony, it would be best to trust her down there —
screams, tries to run away, the Fury lures him with a bottle of brandy, which she holds under his nose

THIRD FURY
Your tongue can't stand it
in your mouth, no more than a fish on dry land!
Fool, you're the man for me, be bold!
Have a look at this bottle and this bell.
It produces a good tone.
Personally, I assume
that fish are mute.
But there is a superstition that, if
you ring a bell by their
ear, they will let slip
a song, surely the shortest
and only one that ever escaped their lips.
I'm the fishwife and need
mute fish for my shop!
Here, have another swig from the bottle.
Fish have to swim.
Go on, go on!
gives him a gentle slap across the face; as he is drunk he falls screaming to the ground

THE FOOL
Man overboard!

Aground!
Aground!

ALL SAILORS *wake with a start, rush to the railing*
Aground?
Aground?
Rudder broken?
Push off with boathooks and spars!
Stuck fast? — Throw out the hook!
Up — what has been caught in the
flukes? A reef! A reef!

THE FOOL *who throughout the scene has left the tiller unattended*
It is surely that lot in the cabin's
fault that we did not avoid
this obstacle!
There are two our ship is unhappy
to carry. — His woman and our
lord!

ALL SAILORS *pulling at a net that the Furies left hanging when they disappeared*
A simpleton you are!
Now the white horses are foaming
again. —
Ahoy! Merry waves because you've
spewed out the garbage?
See what the Devil incarnate
threw at us.
Nets! — Cast! —
Raise — raise —
See it slaver — see it spit —
dripping with water — with spittle —
in the net they find a chopped-off skull covered in seaweed; as they crowd round it falls out of their hands and rolls against the cabin

FIRST SAILOR
What's this? A chopped-off head?
Look at the grin on its face!
Be nice to have that one on, wouldn't it?

THE FOOL
Let's stick it on the
gov'nor's neck.
Him with his pale woman!
Who were sleeping in the cabin while
in such unseemly fashion putting us
in danger.

FIRST SAILOR
Nay, the sea's for everyone —
Is there too little room for you in our boat?
Are you crazy? You should
straightway be struck by a worse fate
for your insolent talk!
Take that round your ears, oaf!
while he is trying to avoid the blows, the Fool stumbles over the skull, finds a gold ring in its teeth, throws the skull into the cabin, and hands the ring to Orpheus

THE FOOL
MY Lord! No trick! No trick!
O golden hope! Gold!
How I was glad
that fortune let me hook something
good. To give it to my Lady.
Who will pop something into my
purse, that would make it feel better!
Brandy I'll buy —

SCENE FOUR

in the cabin. Orpheus and Eurydice on a bench, bleary-eyed

EURYDICE
I dreamed you were going to
throw me out, into the cold, and I
was heavy with your child —

ORPHEUS
— And I that you, thirsting for revenge,
plunge a needle into the heart of the
unborn child —
I hate deceiving night which, groaning,
tosses me from one side to
the other, even more terrible than the first —
Why do you refuse to speak!

EURYDICE
Enough! Enough!
To see such thoughts aimed
at one — you make me
angry and — I feel I am to be a mother —
Have pity!

ORPHEUS
Perhaps I will feel easier, —
if I know — everything — and don't
have to see anything blacker — than black!
— About the nether world!

EURYDICE
No questions! — Oh, could I be more loved!
she stands up when the skull rolls in through the door

ORPHEUS *grabbing her arm fiercely*

Just one thing, do you see — Him
when I am with you?

EURYDICE *sadly*
Stay with me.
Why do we awaken memory!
The ground beneath my feet —
from you I want steadfastness!
amid laughter the Fool passes in the ring, which Orpheus is about to take

EURYDICE
Let what I have still to give you
suffice —

ORPHEUS *in an outburst of anger*
Rather knock over the Gods' table
than that one dish should be lacking!
grabs the ring, reads the inscription, recognizes it
That explains all the effort to keep it secret from me — the silence!
—
The bond broken, the ring?
The inscription scratched out!
Let me read what is left:
"αλλωσ μακαρ"
" — happiness — is another thing!"
harshly
or, hell-cat!
"The other man is happy?"
Unhappiness, it's you I caught! —
You accompanied me with this lie?

EURYDICE
Something has gone bad inside you! —
I can see the dead man's smile again! —
You are just carried away by your happiness,

you call down your unhappiness!
Orpheus tries to throw himself into the sea with Eurydice

ORPHEUS
Back into the past, if that
is your desire!

EURYDICE *threateningly*
And now you hit me! The last straw —
The Other will protect me —.
Could I be more loved? — Listen:
When my remembrance of life above
had been extinguished in the rotting night —
like a tiny candle in a tomb it made
my memory of Orpheus, only
more somber.
Three long years with many nights lasted
the struggle of my conscience with Hades.
That memory alone kept me from the power
of the seducer.
It was Psyche who asked me whether, if I should
be rescued, it would not have been wise to
spare Orpheus the pain.
In the fourth year I had, day and night,
trouble refusing to give myself to him.
And I was often at a loss what to say, to reply.
"Why should I not stand in veils before Hades?"
That was my question.
And Hades: "Virtue likes to go without a veil,
my coy lady, even if Hades' eye sees through it."
Since I was in his hands, how should I
elude him, and I was already about to accept
his proposal, thinking: "I'll go to him."
At that moment, her hands over my
ears, Psyche with her shrewdness held me back,
and answered for me:

"Eurydice holds her virtue fast
and will lose it, when she wants to." —
And in the fifth year —

ORPHEUS
— And in the fifth year?

EURYDICE
— Hades called for me. I could no
longer sleep, nor wake, bombarded
myself: "Go, you timid girl.
You may surely listen, amuse yourself,
for the night still has long to go." —
For already a memory of Orpheus had
faded completely.
And my desire was like a burning flame.
"The one who breathed it into life," I thought,
"is He, Hades, who moves it to and fro."
And Hades embraced me and would not
have had to ask long
for me to unveil myself.
And Hades said: "How is my gentle one to protect herself from Hades,
when she finds her virtue saved by him?"
And I: "I shall go to him!"
But as he was about to drag me inside
his ship, it was Psyche who once
more gave answer, wagging her finger:
"Hey, lovesick girl! It's happiness you need.
Where is there room for that, when curiosity
is in its place?"

ORPHEUS
Once more saved by Psyche's shrewdness —
and in the last year?

EURYDICE
A short time before you came to fetch me, and I
had forgotten you, and the fear that made me shy
away from Hades grown weak, I was
moved by his dull eye, his weary
voice, as He steered toward me in his black boat.
"I have resolved to release you" — a bitter smile —
"By your virtue you have prevailed
over me. Come, I will take you to
Orpheus.
A ring, there, squeezing me, has broken my
heart!"
And then I knew, if I wanted, I could
be free —

ORPHEUS *drawing his knife*
Go on?

EURYDICE
In gratitude, and since I possessed
nothing else, I laughed at his pain,
unloosed my veil! —
"What use has a naked women for these rags!
I have no shame!
For that I laugh, Hades!
You have conquered me!"
Then you came!
Now I leave, because all my courage is gone.
The ground beneath me — from afar I
will call a last farewell to you — to the abode
of shades I flee — to you, Psyche,
sister!
as Eurydice speaks these final words the front part of the ship with the sailors becomes visible once more, the mat falls, from the storm-cloud comes a tempest, whipping the sails.

ALL SAILORS *climbing the shrouds, yelling*
Wind! Wind!
Ahoy! Afloat! We're flying!
Cupid! Thanks! Here have a swig from the bottle!
Otherwise you'll puff up those cheeks too much
and blow the roof off our hut.
Saved! — Wind!
Fire? — Help! — Gone! Gone!
a bolt of lightning strikes, smoke, followed by several more flashes

ORPHEUS *disoriented, waving his knife, rushes out from behind the mat covering the cabin*
Alas! Alas! Mishap!
My happiness! Gone! Unhappiness!
cloud of smoke

ACT THREE

SCENE ONE

Orpheus, in tatters, with careworn, haggard features, appears with a shovel over his shoulder and starts to dig a hole. Hanging above his head is part of the masonry of the vault that has been left standing. It is threatening to collapse, being overgrown with creepers, which will soon pull it down to the ground and its vegetation.

ORPHEUS
A beggar then, so betrayed I am myself.
A waterhole, that's for my skin!
And tanning bark, that's mockery,
because you thought my hide had not been tanned enough
Or was too poor for the deal?
May it not anger you, denizens of the nether world,
if I dare to dig a hole for myself
beside you!
uncovers the fireplace of the house, takes out a handful of ash, weighing it in his hand. A rafter falls, making him look up. Orpheus suddenly recognizes the house as his own

ORPHEUS *cries out*
In this house I lived?
Accursed beam that did not strike me dead!
Is there one stone still standing, a gravestone for me?
O that I cannot perish!
Grubbing in the ashes, like a dog
after bones, for my happiness —
Collapse, o walls! Cave in! Crash down!
For seven years now Charon has been mocking me,
Saying, this night you'll cross, this very night!
finds his broken lyre in the rubble, plays it
Again human voices lamenting amid decay

to deceive me? —
Let furious Cupid's arrow strike me,
that in my song sun and moon, old, old
times, lust and madness, even the image
of Eurydice at last I might curse!

COUNTRY FOLK *coming from the fields*
Listen to the mole!

ORPHEUS
Hey you, rabble!
Pull down this mossy hut,
raze the walls, let the bed grin as empty
as a beggar's purse, fire the roof!
Come down, fire-sprite!
Gravediggers!
Thrust your shovels into my chest!
Tear out my heart, that once, Orpheus against Orpheus,
was divided. Orpheus with Eurydice!
And then off to Hell, damned I was
long ago!
Forests of cloud, start opening up again!
Cascades of mist tumble down, spread
over the many towering crags!
How they renew themselves, in vast infinitude!
Soon to forget Eurydice! Soon you will walk
past me and Orpheus will not question
Eurydice again.

COUNTRY FOLK *pressing closer round him*
Oh, what a splendid catch we've
made with this sourpuss.
Get close and listen to him, that's the thing!
He's not like one of us!
He was the one who started it! Beguiling us, like
a comet's tail, he confused us,

so that we left our village, ran away from
the plowland we were turning over in the sun.
Curious to hear how against nature
he plucked the strings of his lyre,
shot the dart into our flesh.
How love's barb stings!
Feel our hatred, our vengeance!

WOMEN
Make sure you have our fists, if it's for vengeance!
With which we tear apart what we bore!

A DRUNKEN MAN *with a firebrand*
With fire we sear the holes which
love has bitten —

A DRUNKEN WOMAN
Listen! The music!
The sigh is answered by discord!
The lyre of love by the fifes and drums
of tumult, of war!
the rabble has wreaked havoc in the house, started a fire, in their lust for destruction they start a wild dance round Orpheus, who is sitting over his pit, playing. They mock him

A DRUNKEN MAN
Toothless strummer! Lyre and fife rip through
the limbs of the throng!
You men, will you stop clutching aprons?
Tickle his flesh with scorpions
so that, caressed by the touch, he will
leap up and once more, staggering,
try his leg.

WOMEN *tearing at his hair*
Have a good, careful look at your pit.

Our advice is: Get in.
Armed men with celestial ladders are clattering down — quick!
Head first, like that.
To stop you catching
something that will annoy you.
While the wild God of Love races up
and down, kicking his subject people!
warriors on a plundering raid, with musicians

FIRST WARRIOR
What is going on here?

ALL THE COUNTRY FOLK *raising their hats*
They just became a little excited and
that has to be sorted out, sir!

FIRST WARRIOR
You'll soon see how order gets restored!
I'm the most famous, I have
spilled most blood. Make way!
starts tussling with the women over a girl. Falls. Confusion.

THE DRUNKEN WOMAN
Why the scruples!
At first they looked like golden stallions;
but when you get down to it, what do they beget?
Nothing! After trampling the flowery
meadows! Just geldings!
A dead man's fart, that's all your blood-glory is!
Just geldings!

THE WARRIORS
Away with the clubs, set to with your
fists!

the men throwing their weapons away, the warriors their lances, they start to strangle each other, the women helping first one, then another

ALL WOMEN
Bury the scum with dead bodies!
That's immortality!

THE MEN
It's raining blood! Cupid!
Almighty God, is this the end?
Thirst!

THE DRUNKEN MAN
The dogs are drinking blood,
but they also had to put up with
much hardship.
You just have to be hardened.
To be a man means to love your strength!
the ground booms, neighing, furious horses' cries

SOME OF THE WOMEN
In the tangle a mare with runaway
stallions —

OTHERS
The ground must burst open with their stamping —

OTHERS
Who is goading them with stones and whipping?

FIRST WOMAN
The white mare clears the stallions,
unbridled.
See! her belly sweeps the ground.
After her a monster. Half man,

half horse!
Sweat-covered flanks!
Don't stand there gawking!

MEN
The centaur is vying with us.
The strongest step forward!
Increase with lashes the joys of love!
And scatter the torn-off limbs,
blood! In abundance over the earth
not tilled by sweat!
*the bacchanal rages even more wildly, the sound of the lyre still
coming out of the hole, women are carried piggy-back.*

ALL
Dance!
With bites and kisses,
Maenads and madmen!
Leave those that fall
on the ground, wallowing
in filth,
breast to breast,
breeding vermin in the garbage!
Milk mixing with blood!
Decay smoldering in the embers!
Dance past!
Lasses, whip the whirling
boys, but hold on tight
to their necks,
if you're thrown off, you'll be dragged
into the bushes!
Entwine to excess, children!
Rejoice in exultation!
Have mercy on us!
Orpheus is hung up on the site of the fire

SCENE TWO

The scene is arranged so that the tumult is right at the back. An uprooted tree is hanging upside down with its earth-covered roots in the air. Shaking, rumbling, roaring, thunder, silence. The landscape grows paler and paler. Psyche and Cupid, farther off in the distance at first, Psyche glittering, iridescent, Cupid gleaming with gold and dew.

PSYCHE *carrying a gold box, undoes the blindfold over Cupid's eyes and washes them*
Thinking of my own, I forgot Eurydice's happiness.
Thus to the one given into my care
more harm came through my neglect
of duty, through my selfishness, than
from the Furies.
Heedless girl, jealous instrument that I was, I
left the door open to unhappiness.
Myself I robbed of happiness, I blinded the dream.
Cupid, by me the blindfold removed from your eyes!
Remorse would not let me out of its clutches
until in the Underworld I had counted all the dead;
the eyes of all the dead, of all those struck by hate,
which you unceasing sent since you began shooting
arrows of hate from love's bow, those eyes still
open, still wide with fear, I have finally
closed;
until this vessel with my tears o'erflowed.
Washing with this water, I will heal your eyes.

CUPID
I thought I would see bright meadows!
Gray corpses? —

SCENE THREE

out of the pit a smoking column of mist rises, moves along the corpse-strewn ground, as if looking for someone, then stops by the beam, as if it is the right person hanging there: Orpheus

ORPHEUS *swinging*
Dance! Dance!
Hey, all round my life, hey, hey, shades
stealing here from the villages,
streaming here from the burning house.
Eyeball to eyeball, what staring!
From the right and the left, soundlessly —
dogs that don't starve, without barking,
Without biting? —
A horse ran out of the stable,
it didn't want to burn? —
Its damp muzzle!
A slain man in the ditch? —
The chary murderer slipped away just
a short while ago? — Ridiculous!
Again, down we go — Here I am! It's me!
jumps down from the rope, goes into the smoke, striking out with a stick
Yes! I'm tanning my hide.
Just wait and I'll make you a bellows-skin
from it. Cheeky brats!
They come from the world, forget to
run away, when someone's giving up the ghost. —
Standing there, staring, as well?
When someone's stripping off his skin?
Hmm?

WOMAN'S VOICE *from the cloud, harmless*
You're alive.

ORPHEUS
Damned advice!
This or life, what difference does it make. Done for!

WOMAN'S VOICE
Certain?

ORPHEUS
What d'you mean, certain? Certain that I'm done for!
How is it you, mother, know nothing at all about dying;
Can only give birth to children.
You don't understand me any more!

WOMAN'S VOICE
When?

ORPHEUS
Mother! If you're suggesting I
killed myself, tore open the seam
myself, to strip off my skin.
Yes!
Has my blood, all this, not flowed
by my hand? Not?

WOMAN'S VOICE
Don't believe it. You need a good sleep —

ORPHEUS
No! No! Hot work it was, yes! Knife!
But I had a long sleep.
Now I am awake.
Have to stamp out the fire that I had for
singeing-off.
Flame.
Flame-charred man.
A drink?

I'm not a child any more —
Did I perhaps forget to slough some patch of
innocence, on which remained something of the living
man to be overpowered?

WOMAN'S VOICE
Oh, yes!

ORPHEUS
Of course not! That's that! Dead!
And you just get used to it.
Hooray, a devil of a fellow, who spurts blood
when you touch him.
What is there about me that still makes
a human being?
Nothing. You're
just raising the dead!

WOMAN'S VOICE
How wrong it is, rebelling against your mother
who handed you life to taste.
Your grave is the two-foot width
which my hopes stumble over.
It is terrible to be a mortal's
motherly, worn-out vessel.
What is your sorrow?
Child, what have you done?

ORPHEUS
What did I do! I tasted life to
the full! Happiness and unhappiness!
I know enough about them.
You can't light my way any more,
there's nothing new for me to see. Even if I
looked the other way!
Even forgotten thoughts I met

wandering as ghosts, which Hades keeps
in the dark. That no one else ever saw!

WOMAN'S VOICE
To your great detriment!
Just as dogs start barking
whichever way a wanderer
turns. Which constrains him to pass on! —
Even if a look of hate does not dismay us —
May a mother ask her flesh and blood —
"Are you my child? What have you done?" —

ORPHEUS
What is it that you have seen?
Your wisdom! — For days already I have been dead.
Be clearer to me, vision!
What are you, every glance hostile toward me?
Each one neighbor to a thought
which is preparing to denounce me.
To know me better?
To be as dead as I am! To be sure,
you will not change that! Do I look like a
braggart? Ha, ha!
Is the belly piling up even more mud? —

WOMAN'S VOICE
*the column of smoke quivers, sinks down, then rises up again
from the pit*
Alas, just as the flower must perish
for the sake of its fruit,
so for you, my son, does my heart. Alas!
I will tell you your offense:
You wished One dead and
everything fell a-dying.
The living you called dead.
One short word and a Hell full

of meaning!
Orpheus picks up the shovel and starts digging deeper and deeper.

VOICE OF EURYDICE *when the column of smoke rises up again, now rosy pink*
There must be another way
to reach your heart.

ORPHEUS
Orpheus starts to dance, across his shadow
It's not true, or I'd still be the inquisitive
child of the old woman!
What happened to him?
Dance!
Dance! Clear up, merry young things! Pass on!
Don't jump over my shadow! Boo!
Stand still moon! What's the idea?

VOICE OF EURYDICE *her figure becoming clearer*
He is moving closer to the sun, that shines on him,
controlling through him the earth's fruitfulness.

ORPHEUS
I'll fetch him, I'll scratch him out of his lair.
He's to — I want it night!
Sun, withdraw, I say, it's night.
Here on the ground is my hide, stripped off!
Have I kept my word, Hades?

SPIRIT OF EURYDICE *emerging clearly, wrapped in veils*
Tell me, is this the right place to find you?
You have a horrid place here.

ORPHEUS
Not here for a fine show, nor

anywhere else, either.
I don't believe you were so care-
less to come to soothe
misery? I gave my word!
What more do you love to do for me?
Ha! Ha! Who are you?
Only the banished are preceded by a cloud. —

SPIRIT OF EURYDICE
— To give you back a word
that died out — do you remember it —
that was cast out, abandoned
in the cold, in the void, in Hell — Eurydice! —

ORPHEUS
That became foreign to me, breathed out —

SPIRIT OF EURYDICE
You, the thought, my unhappiness that had
dragged, chained, compelled me —
to come, to cast it at you, like a stone
wrapped in rags.

ORPHEUS
You! I am deceased and your doing
is not my child.

SPIRIT OF EURYDICE
If you are now only a shade
there must be some reason you are
cunningly spread abroad to blacken
my outing.
Wherever you touch me, I turn moldy.
So be it!
Surely law obtains in the worst case?
Alas! Orpheus, my life!

ORPHEUS
Go! Go! I say. You should not require anything
of Orpheus.
I say! One more request, what is that?
What kind of bond is it binding man and wife together. — Our
own imagination!
Which makes fools of us!
What was there about you, about me, beyond what our
imagination scrawls on dreams belonging to all
women and men, as nights to the day.
To be thought One above the Many,
What a fraud!
And how I went along with it.
When I thought of you, my heart stood still,
my throat went dry, I turned pale.
Can a dead man have rights and
wrongs, like the living?

SPIRIT OF EURYDICE
See me on my knees before you!
O my debtor, give me my right posthumously,
since I had to die without it!
Alas, Orpheus! Life!

ORPHEUS
Spirit of despair
do you try me still?
O aftertaste of the cup that
made me thirst.
Scoop, scoop up, o ever empty hand,
my hand.
Grip, grip round the rim. Hands!
We have killed, ripped off our flesh.
Dancing hours of love with our naked memories,
which die before we begin to remember them.
Dancing over the corpse-bed between us!

SPIRIT OF EURYDICE
Yes! Yes! I want to embrace you once again,
so lovingly that every girl shall envy me.
Only — oh, in the face of sin my courage
deserts me — do not invite me to a spectacle,
you double dealer, here before curious eyes,
full of putrefaction and naked?
Now at last let me go.
Spare me in the end at least.
Hear then, when you have had me enough,
will you leave me?
Willingly accord my abused heart its due?
Yes? You must do that, mustn't you?
If you called me, you will do that! —
You will finally release me?

ORPHEUS
Let us shake our hearts, our heads,
our hands, our rags, the mist! —
What falls out? A fortune card:
"The one shall ever find happiness in the other?" —
For, mine, I must ask,
as long as this eye is open, see answer in yours!

SPIRIT OF EURYDICE
You invite me once more — I can't go on!

ORPHEUS
There from the beam see me hang, the fire
in the hearth below like all our woes.

SPIRIT OF EURYDICE
The wolf has a different opinion of the lamb
than the latter has of the beast that has eaten it.
Have I not done enough for you? — Here I am —
nothing left any more!

Soon you will rot from the blood you thirst after.
throwing off her veil, naked
A naked woman comes before the court, lacking
sufficient modesty any longer
to cover rape with lean hands.
The veil tear!
The corpse bare!
Proves how tortured I am!
How rough you are!
One corner of my being, as we all
do, with modesty from your staring
eyes I tried to hide — as you
reached out unsuspecting — in that short span I
used my advantage, fleeing backwards
to death, with a handful of ashes I
blinded you!
In those ash-reddened eyes no mirror trapped Eurydice
ever again!

ORPHEUS
Lustful no more is the image of the sun,
to burn its way through my red, empty sockets
into my heart, there unleashing storms —
hm — and do you know —
nor from the ashes beneath does fire belch up
clouds!
Don't you remember who forgot the fire in the hearth?
The centaur!
The pyre for one scorched by lightning!
Where the angry goddess burnt him,
when he yearned to kiss her naked flesh
behind the cloud!

SPIRIT OF EURYDICE
You respect nothing! How many things, ere now, —
yielding is the mother of invention — I allowed

to be done to me, as to a sacrificial beast.
Until, strangled by my lord, I fell to my knees.
Mad with happiness, into Orcus after Eurydice
Orpheus threw himself.
What arrogance!
To wrest from death a forfeit victim!
Still from sleep rapaciously withholding her?
Where hope is not, who will hope for a delusion?
How long have you been digging? Are you still?
Each spadeful vaults me in more tightly!
Enough! Happiness, unhappiness squeezed dry!
Enough!
Soon all you will see, Eurydice joining
the flames of the departed,
leaving in smoke, descending —
out of the hole that Orpheus has finally finished digging, from the hearth, flames shoot to and fro. The fire appears to fertilize itself, multiplying everywhere, giving birth anew. In a small blue opening Psyche's head appears, with a heavenly radiance, takes the lyre out of the flames, the blue disappears with her head, but the lyre begins to lament. When Orpheus tries to catch Eurydice, a swarm of the departed imitate the lover's capers in a macabre dance

ORPHEUS
Oh, smoldering in the fire is your face, hiding?
Come here! I'll leap out of this tinder, you in my arms,
save us from the gulf, which, blazing all around,
yawns —

SPIRIT OF EURYDICE
— Death is everywhere our fate —
Try, here a hand?

ORPHEUS
Hold on! I'll not let you go!

Orpheus and Eurydice 161

Got you!

SPIRIT OF EURYDICE
Have you managed —

ORPHEUS *dancing with Eurydice*
With fiendish delight I confess:
I hate you!
My deed — Hades — Death outwitted!
You, it's you, here, you did not neglect
to grin in my dimming eye! Dance! Dance!
And see now. This Hades did not let you live!
You here! Victory! I will not let you die!
Howl, Hell! Burning! —
What have I done, cursing you my love?!
Spew out, tongue, it hates itself!
That is more — Me! I deserve it!
For I loved her, loved! — Love!
Do you hear, Hades?
Silence. Orpheus collapses to his knees
A murderer directs his confession at the spot
where the blood comes from, everything!
Evil men, plagued by conscience, think out loud:
"I remember a night resembling that."
Whew!
— To forget the thing I loved! — A self was
at work inside me and rocked in a wave
of blood One that resembled you —
with a mad laugh
As long as what lives in there was secret.
Until from the mouth screams flow to Those
who are no more!
Flying from lips to ear,
a burnt smell — glows.
A musty smell — suffocates
until with terror it fills death to the edges. —

Behind love unto death lurks —
hate!

SPIRIT OF EURYDICE
Since love is so nonsensical, then
death must mean abandoning our selves?

ORPHEUS *choking with laughter*
Mother, ooh! How does it go —
Thou shalt not kill — not kill —
*Eurydice tries to smother Orpheus' mad laughter by pressing
both hands against his cheeks, lacing them round his neck. It
lasts a long time. The lyre still whimpers. Something dark swishes
in the half-light. A piercing cry from a bird, then one from its
pursuers*

SPIRIT OF EURYDICE
You breathed the fire,
it burns you. Centaur!
Now — you are ashes!
Thus in the last battle embracing,
full of horror,
for the last kiss, from Orpheus' stiffened jawbones
finally I loose myself free.
Monotonous song of the earth —
Whatever we encircle, always happiness is different —
Is it hatred, such love?
This longing —
the darkness is rent.

EPILOGUE

Psyche becomes visible on the spot where Eurydice led the dance of the spirits and faded with them.

PSYCHE *with a bundle made up of ears of grain, tear-bedewed roses, tulips, and lilies in her lap, the lyre in her arm; wakes up, stretches out her hands toward the dawn twilight, the distance*
No one here?
With the stolen kiss
you slipped so quietly away
that I just went on sleeping?
O you hours, intoxicating rivers;
Singing, laughing, crying still sound in my ears —
puts her hands over her ears, laughing, as if she were being tickled there
Oh, it's you, not you my dream-darling —
What — you thought — thought, quick,
you could hide here a while?
rubbing her eyes
Close by me I see a railing
near to the light,
in the air above it a veil was fluttering,
yours, Cupid!
It was yesterday!
Playing.
You were instructing Psyche in visions,
to which,
like all those jealous of feeling's
license, she was listening with mixed emotions. —
And one thing did not meet with my approval,
that Cupid lured Psyche behind the lilacs!
"Look, Psyche,
tie a blindfold over my eyes."
And you were naked,
with my hand I could feel it.

Straightway you whispered,
"Oh Psyche, it is not a blindfold
you are tying, no, you are tying me."
And I thought the blindfold over your eyes
did not suit you, so that even I
no longer recognized you, when, from the bow,
on which love's arrows are stretched,
I saw a whole quiver of hatred menacing me!
And then you laughed,
"Psyche!
What have you done!"
One hour later you were free to leave me;
after the — previously — poisoned arrows
every fiber with bliss had scratched.
Tenderly my hand I wave to you,
because the kisses' marks I find!
Cupid! I'm not so frightened any more
as I was - then!
Away we go!
strews flowers over the field. Girls wake up and pick them to make a posy

CHORUS OF YOUNG WOMEN
Away we go!
Impelled by the voice
which consists of one word — Hope!
Hope, a thousandfold echo sighing
with every blade in the wind,
as, piercing the earth's crust,
with a shudder of profound rapture
the grass feels itself rising toward the
light of Heaven.

PSYCHE *stepping into the black bark tied up at the bank*
Let eternal light shine upon them —

CHORUS OF YOUNG MEN *waking up, rising from the ground*
Hope! Seed
springing up out of the night,
is it ready yet for reaping?

PSYCHE
Awake!
One more bloody bolt trembles,
plunges into the sea.
And now the sun casts its infinite
radiance over the sleeping night —

CHORUS OF OLD PEASANT WOMEN *running anxiously to the young folk*
Beware!
Like Conception and Death,
Hope couples with Fear.
Fear and Hope reach out to
the glittering sun,
and cannot shake it.

amid laughter, the young girls garland the men with flowers

CHORUS OF YOUNG WOMEN
Shall we, you rogues, exchange flowers with you?
The roses in our cheeks awoke after the first
kiss, when we found on the dewy blossoms
your traces everywhere!

PSYCHE *playing the lyre, the boat sails away*
Tears on the blood of their maiden's cheeks
the dream bequeathed
to the startled sleepers —

CHORUS OF YOUNG MEN *clashing with their goblets, merry shouts*
Yes, that's how it was!

When Cupid softly slipped away
Psyche awoke with tears!

PSYCHE *the ship disappearing from view, lyre*
I was — closest — to him!
I love you all! —

CHORUS OF YOUNG MEN
The thousand-tiered sun approaches —
and one last time, before its radiance,
Psyche casts her eyes back —

CHORUS OF YOUNG WOMEN
— joyous as the lark
worshiping the sun.
all kneel down.

COMENIUS

Play 1936-38/1972

168 *Comenius*

CHARACTERS, in order of appearance

SHYLOCK, Jew at the court of the Emperor Ferdinand
FERDINAND, later Emperor of the Holy Roman Empire
CAPUCHIN MONK
VALERIANUS, Dominican monk, later Inquisitor in Bohemia
LEOPOLD OF TYROL, Ferdinand's brother
DRABIK, showman
EMPRESS ELEONORE FROM MANTUA, Ferdinand's wife
COLONEL GORDON of the Spanish Guards
CZECH AND GERMAN KNIGHTS
COUNT WALLENSTEIN, Ferdinand's field marshal
KATHARINA, his wife
CANDLEMAKER
THE WOOD-FOLK
AMOS COMENIUS, taught religion in schools before becoming Bishop of the Moravian Brethren
HANNAH, little Jewish girl, called Christl as Comenius' foster-child
CHILDREN
SKRBENSKY, Moravian lord
ZEROTIN'S WIFE
ZEROTIN, Moravian lord and protector of the Unity of Moravian Brethren
TRCKA, Bohemian lord
LORDS AND LADIES, Bohemian, Moravian and German
COLONEL WITH SOLDIERS
BROTHERS AND SISTERS OF THE COMMUNITY IN FLIGHT
DE GEERT, Comenius' favorite disciple
AXEL OXENSTIERNA, Swedish Chancellor
QUEEN CHRISTINA OF SWEDEN
COUNT SPORCK FROM BOHEMIA
REMBRANDT VAN RIJN
HENDRIJKE STIFFELS
CIVIC GUARD
SPANISH GUARDS, VOICES FROM THE PEOPLE
TWO CITIZENS, ONLOOKERS AT THE PROCESSION

LACKEYS, HERALDS, NOBLES, CLERGY, OFFICERS
CHILDREN, SERFS, SOLDIERS
PEASANT GIRLS

The events take place around the time of the Thirty Years' War of Religion, in the countries that were chiefly afflicted by that catastrophe: Bohemia, Moravia, Germany, Austria

ACT ONE

SCENE ONE

A corridor-like chamber in the Hofburg in Vienna with a row of doors, before each of which stands a Spanish Guard; marble busts in the spaces between them; on the table a map of the Spanish-Habsburg Empire. The personal barber of Archduke Ferdinand, the brother of the Emperor, Matthias, is standing looking at the bust of Augustus.

SHYLOCK 'Tu, felix Austria, nube' — While others make war, Austria makes marriages. By my fathers, for us Jews it's enough to be able to trace our origins back to the first man and woman! It's different with these gentiles. Here, in his Roman toga and crowned with his laurel wreath, is Gaius Julius Caesar, one of Our distant relatives — according to the Habsburg family tree. It's on Caesar's descent from Aeneas, the exile who founded Rome after the fall of Troy, that Our claim to the Holy Roman Imperial Crown is based. And doesn't legend trace Aeneas' genealogy back to a nymph the heathen god Jupiter took to his bed? So it was only logical Caesar should have himself declared god while he was still alive, and there's still an echo of that on the debased ducats of Our Most Serene Majesty — Imperator Dei gratia! *takes out his large pocket watch, puts it to his ear and shakes his head; stands hesitating outside one of the closed doors*

GUARD *lowers his pike before him*

SHYLOCK *starts, puts his watch back into his doublet; bowing to the guard* My reverence, Sir Veteran. Could have taken you for a monument left over from the religious wars. That must mean the ironsides outside the next door is also a kind of unknown soldier deserving of our reverence because he gave up the ghost in the last war, the one that was fought to put an end to war. A Yid's not afraid of ghosts.

GUARD Pasen!

SHYLOCK Move along, should I? Even those who have to stand at attention move with the times. A clown! No idea that the war's over. Was it the ticking of my little timepiece that had you up in arms? It's not the sound of revolt against the imperial purple, oh no. Even the hour-hand of my little chronometer is not allowed to stand still, not even in the Vienna Hofburg. *going to the map and pointing to where Spain is drawn on it* . . . my memory does not deceive me. Was it not in Our Spain where the sun never set? The sands of time had run out for the widow, when, with the death of Philip the Handsome, time stood still and the sun never rose again for her. Here it is on the map. There. The Escorial. *in weary tones* I was still a child when I saw the unforgettable features of Joanna, grandam of our most noble ruling dynasty, through a pane of glass in her leather coffin — blessed be her memory. Forty-seven long years she was kept prisoner, first by her royal father, then by her royal mother, and finally by her own son, Charles the Fifth, who wanted to unite the world in everlasting peace and ended up in a monastery; she refused to change her shift, ate her meals off the unswept floor like a wild animal, and they took her children away from her. Not for parents, nor for husband, nor child, nor people did she mourn, but reserved her unreasoning sorrow for the loss of her crown. Hand out money and favors and you're one of the great and good, that's the way it is with historians. One sees history this way, the other tells it differently. Some make our grandam a houri, others a saint. The Spanish people, however, call her *Juana, la loca*, 'Joanna the Mad.' My memory does not deceive me. I tell of the things I have seen, even when no one is listening. You have to do something for entertainment. Who can sleep here, where the sands have run out and time stands still, just as it does in Spain? Will they start striking my fathers down again here as well, expelling them and burning them under the Holy Inquisition? Why shouldn't we have that here too? People are wondering, for — don't make me laugh! — who would willingly lend money — I ask you! — to the bankrupt Empire? On the other hand, who can understand the caprices of our rulers, they're a race apart. You have to work out a *modus vivendi*, a compromise, half for me, half for thee, King Solomon said so ages ago. So, the Jews for us, the money for the Empire! By the God of our fathers, what does a Jew do in a situation like this? I'm going to see the rabbi, let him decide.

The door closest to the auditorium opens and Ferdinand, a little red-haired mannikin dressed in black, with a goatee, a shabby doublet, and threadbare velvet hose, is standing before the Jew, looking at him in a way that suggests he is looking right through him at invisible worlds.

FERDINAND *almost inaudibly* I heard a quite excellent remark, but here it's forbidden to think.

Guard, on guard outside this door, lowers his pike between the two as the barber is about to enter the door

SHYLOCK If this iron windmill only had human hands it would be easier to talk to it. *stands still because an eerie procession is approaching from the end of the corridor*

FERDINAND *standing in the open room before Titian's portrait of Charles V* The son of the madwoman, Charles, fifth of that name, the emperor who wanted to unite the world, withdrawn to a monastery of his own free will. *lost in thought* The lands of the empire where the sun never set had been bled so white that he couldn't pay for a requiem mass for his mother. A new spirit, that's what's needed for the continuity of the concept of the Holy Roman Empire. Not even my barber will give anything for this head, if we don't succeed in bringing these rebellious ideas, that are subverting humanity, under political control. The revolt of the Utraquists in Bohemia, the Calvinists in Hungary and the Lutherans in the Austrian lands is spreading like a forest fire. The mutinous protestants are at the gates of Vienna. Rudolf, my imperial cousin in Prague, childless, head full of astrology and mechanical inventions,

Comenius 173

had to abdicate in favor of Matthias; Matthias had to flee Prague and sign the imperial edict in Vienna, according to which his Majesty submits to the supervision of the defenders of the revolutionary Protestants. Even in the Hofburg in Vienna there are assassins lurking. Is it Matthias who sends them out, to save his own life? I am worried about what it might mean . . . *the procession has reached the open door, a bell sounds, servants with various articles, guards* . . . it may well be worse to know. It is strange that on such days one is so calm, without having any reason to be . . .

COLONEL OF THE GUARDS *to the Jew; the servants hand him a white shirt.* You're to shave his beard, Yid!

FERDINAND *unmoved, speaking in a drawling voice* This chamber has a special acoustic, the ear of the ailing Emperor. I see I'm to be washed, to be dressed in clean clothes. Does it mean the bell was to announce my last hour? The hour God is granting me to unite this age. That would take superhuman powers, it is beyond a mere mortal. *pauses, looks at the floor for minutes on end, the floorboards creak under his foot* It's Maundy Thursday. That means the execution can take place the day before the crucifixion. The whole of Vienna will be on its feet *in a whisper* apart from me. *unresisting, he allows himself to be sat in the chair and have the shirt put over him. The Jew begins to shave off his beard* Is our imperial brother's executioner already in the building? All my moist eye misses is love, sunshine and freedom, which is worth more than all the gold my Spanish forefather tore out of the entrails of the Indians. You have cheated me of everything, cousin Matthias, out of fear for your crown. Neither the consecrated oil on your head, nor your hypocrisy, indecision and outmoded particles of faith will save the Empire. Yid! If only your knife were more sure than my head. Character reveals itself in the condemned cell: a predatory salmon boldly tugs at the line, the fainthearted loach dies the moment it takes the fly. *the servants put bread and wine, a last meal for the condemned man, on a small table. Ferdinand proudly waves it away* Out of compassion you even mix an opiate in the prisoner's wine, but give the food to the hangman! Sensuous pleasure ill becomes the last hour of a poor sinner who is about to be hanged. *the Jew hands him a mirror, Ferdinand looks in the mirror; imperiously* I am not yet a mask, dead, with its jaws bound up. Let the Emperor hear my last word. Tell him, tell Matthias I hold nothing against him, not even that which seemed unforgivable. Tell him he could not frighten me. *more violently* I would not have rested content until I had the crown of Bohemia; now all I ask, even if I have to open Saint Wenceslas' vault in Prague to get it, is the cross on the crown with the thorn from Christ's crown enclosed in it. But with that thorn as a goad I would have had the opportunity of ruling Europe with a strong hand. My pulse is beating faster. To make the whole of mankind feel what I was suffering, that would be a successful escape from my tortured existence. Jew? There is only one day left that counts now . . . Shylock, do you understand the significance of the evil image staring at me out of the mirror? Is it me? *looking round suspiciously* No one should pay much attention to the words this mask stammers at the moment it is preparing to be a better self . . . *softly, aside* instead of the mortal coil of the man looking in this mirror. *drops the mirror, disheartened.* My sins are for the ear of my confessor alone.

SHYLOCK *during this he has wiped the soap off Ferdinand's face; he starts, giving himself away* The mask falls, oh God of my fathers! *correcting himself* Your beard is all I have taken, that was my task, not your confession, that is not my business. *finishes shaving him*

FERDINAND *taken aback, holds the mirror in front of the Jew's face* Barber, can you read the future? Look!

SHYLOCK *succumbing to Ferdinand's suggestive power, in a strained voice, ambiguous* No mortal's voice has spoken the law governing the future, no lips that once clung to a mother's hand can pass that judgment on humanity. *aside* A face like this can eat even the Jews into starvation. After all, our existence depends on trade, so beware! I can see that if I were to use my reason to give advice here, I would not be long for this life myself.

FERDINAND *eagerly* Go on! I am waiting; do not be afraid to speak your mind.

SHYLOCK *shudders, expressing himself more clearly* If the sign speaks the truth and this face should come to power, you, noble lord, would happily break humanity on the wheel if you knew of no other way of freeing them from their errors. Mankind stands at a turning point. More and more enlightened in our daily labors, thanks to the Greek teachings of the great Aristotle, with the commentary by our Spanish rabbi Maimonides, we are developing a belief in reason, which God gave us to preserve humanity from fearful night. But the harsh "no" from these lips to all liveliness reduces the spirit of enlightenment to nothing more than a bad dream, the effect of too much schnapps. Even if that were the sum of what I can read in this face, I would have learnt in good time to fear the future.

After the Jew has finished his task, the lackeys help Ferdinand up from his chair; Ferdinand is taken with a cramp and spews into the barber's bowl.

FERDINAND The Peace of Augsburg lies heavy on my stomach. The compromise of religious freedom with those who are seeking the total reform of the Church. In the Empire one hundred years of the Holy Roman Empire are going up in smoke! I feel sick!

SHYLOCK *packing up his instruments and bowing* I ask your forgiveness for having taken the liberty of interpreting the future.

FERDINAND *shakes himself, jumps up, calls after the Jew as he is going through the door* Take the evil image with the redbeard that pursues me out of my sight, put it in your box with your instruments. Will Providence give me enough time to pray my soul clean? Doors slamming open and shut! Clouds in the sky, red clouds!

There! A door is opening! Have a look, is it safe? *Ferdinand rushes to the prayer-stool with the crucified Christ hanging over it, on the wall the crown of thorns towers over the Habsburg crown* Call my confessor! *again the death-knell tolls, while the monk, his steps inaudible, strides along the corridor, to the inner chamber; Ferdinand, scared to death, buries his face in his praying hands; louder and louder* As if some celebration were being interrupted, not a human soul. Can you see no one in the corridor, will you swear to it? *suddenly, to the guards, who remain mute* A shadow! Slipping along the wall! Is it the hangman? No! In my entrails I can feel it. It's the Capuchin monk. The one with the clubfoot that even Satan hides. How I waited for the new spirit . . . on the horizon of the new age, the tide is ebbing. Monk! Ghost! Reminder of my sin! Do I see you survive? The sign! Your silence is unbearable! If you are not dead to the salvation of your own soul, my death throes must move you.
the bell continues to toll If you cannot pray with me, then at least howl, whimper, cry, laugh. *thunder of cannon. The Habsburg crown falls off the wall.* You, monk, did you see? A sign from above?
The monk, his shadow falling across the scenery, picks up the crown from the floor and puts it on Ferdinand's head as, stunned, he gradually comes back to reality.

FERDINAND *his voice hoarse with emotion* A coup d'état! Matthias no longer needs to sue the heretics for peace. He is resting in peace. Treachery! Do you hear, you men? I am not the guilty one! I cannot be a Christian and at the same time have murdered the dwarf who rules — ruled in Austria. *puts his hands to his neck, as if he were trying to free himself from a noose; in a calm voice* These my hands are not red with blood. Matthias *gloating* can no longer hear . . . he will never know. *to the monk* What does it say in the catechism, Father? "Thou shalt not kill!"

EMISSARIES OF THE REBEL COUNT THURN *press into the room, take hold of Ferdinand* Murderer of freedom! Jesuit puppet! All the lands are in revolt. The Hofburg is in our hands. Surrender!
The sound of hooves is heard in the courtyard; the chamber is stormed by cavalry led by Leopold of Tyrol; Thurn's emissaries flee.

FERDINAND My brother Leopold from the Tyrol! I did not pray for a miracle in vain. *they embrace*

CAPUCHIN MONK *raises his right arm in homage, servants kneel before Ferdinand, the guards salute with their pikes and swords*

COLONEL OF GUARDS Hail Ferdinand!

SCENE TWO

Emperor Ferdinand in disguise, coming out of the Crypt of the Capuchin Church into the daylight. He is emaciated, plagued with nausea. Shylock is waiting for him outside the iron gate.

EMPEROR *sighing* We feel sick. We've eaten our fill just once at dinner and that does it.

SHYLOCK So it did not soothe my gracious Lord Ferdinand to see for himself that his late lamented imperial cousin was safely interred in the monks' church? The fright must have affected your sympathetic nerve, and now we see the result: the philosophy of an upset stomach which is both an infectious and pernicious disease of the Caesars. In future the well-being of the Empire may depend on what you eat and drink. As a doctor, I recommend Carlsbad plums for Your Majesty's imperial indigestion.

EMPEROR *shaking himself* The scene-change that became history was too abrupt, even for the theater. From Hades to a God-given throne — it's a miracle. As a confessional secret it will remain hidden in the ear of the mute monk whom God has given the power to bind and to loose.

SHYLOCK It turns your stomach. The air is foul down there. Come up here and join the merry Viennese. *Shooing away a cat* A cat may look at a king . . . *making a way for the Emperor through the throng of people without sight, ears, noses, arms, who are standing outside the monastery with their begging bowls, shouting:* A copper for a cripple, in the name of God!

SHYLOCK Make way for a high-born gentleman, or rather, for one who, thanks to divine justice, has risen so high that everything in the Empire has fallen down from its natural place. Make way in the ranks of the fallen there!

EMPEROR *frightened by the crowd, holds on tight to the Jew*
I feel queasy again. The people stink like the bears' cage in the Hofburg. *with a sudden movement turns away from the street and the cries of rejoicing, back to the crypt, where the coffins can be seen illuminated by candles* I am in no mood to join in the people's rejoicing. The courtyard in the Hofburg did not echo with laughter, all that came to the prisoner's window was the dull tread of the guards. *looking back at the crypt* Now you are resting in peace, cousin Matthias.

SHYLOCK Your Majesty is suffering from the Imperial Idea, which one could call the German disease, just as syphilis is the French disease and rickets the English disease, from which only the noble lords get fat bellies. The smallest digit, yes, even a naught, will go mad if the one leaps over others to the head of the number. Let us employ our reason and look at it this way: Your Majesty is suffering from the fact that your head is seen as the head of the Empire. Now let's do some sums: for example, one murderer surely remains one murderer, even if only God knows of his crime. And two murderers remain two, yes? And three are no more than three. Isn't that correct? So, how many murderers must the head command for wrong to turn into right and murder into legitimate warfare, a holy war in the name of God, for the good of the people? The divine commandment has become a syllogism. The crafty monk would have greeted you with "Hail Caesar," instead of with "In the name of the Lord," if you gave to the Church that which is the Church's: monasteries, lives, serfs. The pious bride of the Lord rejoices as she clutches hard cash to her chest. Even if money came from the Archfiend, you couldn't tell by the smell, as they say in Rome. But peace is what the Emperor should make, that's what the Yid advises.

EMPEROR *to the Jew, at a loss what to do* How gentle, like endless rain, does the chorus of peace sound. Peace! Peace! the pious believers gabble their creed in harmony with our creditors. Of the German lords, none is ready to help until he has cash in hand. The Protestant electors don't want a united Empire and get France and the Catholic League to attack us, and they say the secret commissioners of the Holy See are already traversing the Empire to estimate the Holy Father's future income. Therefore We, too, will have to uphold Our authority with the sword, as did Our late predecessor. There is no peace, except for the dead. Have you heard anything from your people, Shylock?

SHYLOCK *shrugging his shoulders* My gracious lord Emperor is burying his head in the sand like the ostrich in the desert, refusing to believe the Empire is withered, bankrupt, ruined. The exchanges in Amsterdam, London, Genoa and Paris are speculating on the money collected. If my Lord Ferdinand of the Divine Right does not make peace, then we will refuse the Empire the means to continue arming, that's what the Chosen People say, Ferdinand offers no security for our money.

EMPEROR *stamping his foot* The Jew, the usurer, cheating Our people, clipping Our coins, drags Our honor through the mire, and still the ungrateful race will not be prevailed upon?

SHYLOCK *cautiously pressing home his advantage* My gracious lord Emperor is surprised to learn that my brothers abroad prefer a rational policy, and withdraw from the court as soon as their financial commitments there threaten to become bad business? Their complaints are unjust? When the whole of Christianity, in the modern world, is weighed in the balance of justice, the Jews are the pointer, the frail needle on the balance beam. But what has, apparently, been weighed in the balance and found wanting is brute force, that is a fact of the modern world that reason is learning to take into account. O God of my fathers! Money is a clean trade to be in, you don't get blood on your hands, and it frees the Chosen People from their slavery to the Emperors. Israel has bought back its birthright with money. The Gentiles, be they Papists or Protestants, cannot see the difference between the empire of force and that of reason. *with a mocking laugh* It is a different world now from the old one, where gold was useless, as unprofitable as the lives of the Indians, who didn't recognize its value and gave it to the horse-soldiers of His Spanish Majesty, my gracious lord Ferdinand's ancestors, in exchange for the tidings of the gospel of love. *laughs and rises up menacingly from his servile posture* Shylock the Jew thinks a turning-point in the history of mankind has arrived. If the Emperor insists on steering the ship of state against the current of time, forcing it upriver and back into the streams, all the way to the source, it may well be that, at the end of the day, the idea of empire will dissolve into thin air, and from the Jew, instead of how to pass and carry out sentence, the Emperor will learn how to do his sums and think straight.

The Emperor is about to hit him, but the two are already surrounded by the populace. The iron gate to the vault is slammed shut, the Emperor with the Jew going up to the New Market. High-gabled, half-timbered Viennese houses; in the street a crowd of soldiers in ceremonial dress, with brightly colored sashes and feathers in their caps, girls in their bodices decked out in jewelry and fashionable hairstyles. Bishop in a purple cassock, followed by Dominicans. Noblemen on horseback with dogs and runners, peasants, craftsmen. All are pressing forward to see the ceremonial procession of the young Empress.

SHYLOCK *guiding the Emperor through the crowd* Make way please, ladies and gentlemen.

VOICE FROM THE PEOPLE Hurrah for the young Empress!

1st CITIZEN *in conversation* She's in for a big surprise. So far all she's seen is the Emperor's wedding-ring, they put it on her finger in the grotto of the Virgin in Lourdes, where the miracles have been happening.

2nd CITIZEN That's something I've been asking myself, whether the prayers of that fiery woman from Mantua will succeed in squeezing a son and heir from the Habsburg family tree.
with a laugh 'Tu felix Austria nube' — Austria making her marriages — that's why the people have come to gawk.

1st CITIZEN Listen to the people rejoicing, the Viennese music, the sweet tones of the fiddlers. A damned soul from hell would fall in love if he heard the blandishments of the famous Viennese heart. The bells of St. Stephen's are ringing out in praise. There's more than one was tempted in good faith by the exuberance of the populace of Vienna to misuse the power the people had given him. But it's very capricious, is our dear vox populi, and in a trice it can be hissing out its hatred.

2nd CITIZEN Peace is the magnet that will bring money back into our coffers after the war.
The first carriages of the Imperial procession with retinue drive past.

EMPEROR I'm not interested in seeing the Empress drive past in the royal carriage. The marriage is being forced on me, by the gentlemen of the privy council as well as by the man in the street; they're already thinking of the succession. *full of suspicion and mistrust, he tries to hear everything people are saying about him.*

2nd CITIZEN All the people want is peace, that's why they were foolish enough to go over to the Protestant faith, because the Roman faith turned a deaf ear to them.

SHYLOCK Gracious lord Ferdinand, that entertaining man over there is giving expression to more of the public opinion that has been suppressed up to now.

DRABIK *outside one of the fairground booths; he is using a jumping jack as a ventriloquist's dummy, which he pretends is reading from a pamphlet. The onlookers make fun of his act* Oh dear, look at me, poor honest Fritz, who's supposed to lay golden eggs for the Emperor. What with warfare, the grain tribute, timber dues, the great tithe, the little tithe, salt tax, market tolls, seal duty, marriage dues, petition stamps, poultry taxes, my last cow's long since been taken from my stall. And now new war levies! What are you doing to the Empire, Holy Roman Emperor? *wailing* Grain, hops, rape, flax, turnips, fruit, all trampled by the military. The people are eating grass, the less devout among them are already eating the flesh of their own children. Hunger, plagues — the charnel houses have long been full to overflowing. Poor Fritz has been flogged to death, he's been spied on, interrogated, strung up, broken on the wheel, he's been cheated and robbed. If we don't get a miracle instead of new hostilities, then you can take my word for it, Lord, the German Empire'll shoot itself dead as a doornail!

PEOPLE You're an agitator! You promised us a novelty. Come on, let's see Fritz shit ducats or give us our money back. Show us something new!

DRABIK *making the puppet jiggle up and down, pulling coins out of its backside and showing them to the crowd* Look, good people, on the coin, the head of the new Emperor Ferdinand.

SHYLOCK *steps on one, puts it between his teeth and bites it, to see if it is genuine; in a mocking aside* The false twins from the imperial mint! Oi veh! Once upon a time, in exchange for your ducat you could get several pounds of meat, a hundred ells of good cloth, a bushel of grain. Today all you get for it is a scrap of paper from the Imperial Bank, to keep your feet warm, if you still happen to possess a pair of wooden clogs . . . Huh!

EMPEROR *to Drabik, with a stunned expression* My good man, in the old days we were more tolerant, but with the rebel Count Thurn at the gates of the Hofburg in Vienna, and Ourself given up by Leopold, Our brother from the Tyrol — and likewise, fortunately, by Our cousin Matthias, the late Emperor — for Us progress means reshuffling the cards. Crude swindles were all right for the knights of old, but now the Jew keeps a close eye on us, on our Lutheran brothers as well as on the Emperor! To satisfy the people, silver from the Bohemian mines will be added to the coinage. *playing with the insignia of the Golden Fleece, which the people draw back from. Drabik falls to his knees. The Emperor gives him a kick, knocking him over. In control of himself once more, craftily* Hey, you lout, stand up. The new spirit requires the ruler to find the ear of the people. Tell us some more of what they call public opinion. Get on with it! Where do you come from?

DRABIK *in a low voice* Bohemia. The place where a teacher said, "How can a servant of Christ allow himself to be king of a heathen Roman empire over the people, over which Christ alone is king? Without laws backed up by the threat of the executioner, no king could rule. Thus are the laws of man."

EMPEROR *sounding him out further* If that's the latest news you have from Bohemia, then let me, inexperienced prince that I am, tell you to your paling face that the Viennese scum thinks no differently from the Bohemian dregs. We have heard that in Bohemia they preach in the mother tongue, and that the communion chalice of the heretic Hus is chiseled into the wall over the door of every Utraquist church. You forget that the Emperor is the temporal arm of the Church.

DRABIK *cowering on the ground* Is the Emperor no longer satisfied with the natural respect of his subjects, as from time immemorial?

EMPEROR Truly, ruling is no longer the imperial passion it once was. It is turning into a war of ideas since printed books became popular, paper is long-suffering and the means justify the end. Good! We understand the common people want to learn to read and to write? Newspapers! If that is the case, then we, too, want to promote the reformation of minds through science and method. No more talk of force, my good man, reason's the thing now. But people shouldn't blow Us out, like the candles in church once mass is over. *trumpets are heard, aside* Blackest melancholy seizes one when one hears how even in Vienna agitation against the House of Habsburg goes unpunished. In Bohemia the trees still have plums hanging from them instead of you . . . *to the Jew* We scorn the Viennese rabble. A standing army, equipped with the new firearms like the Spanish, that would be our answer, but, because of the uprising in the Netherlands, Our cousin in Spain needs all his men, and We lack money! France, England, Hungary, Savoy, even the Holy Father together with the Sultan of Turkey are all against Habsburg. *taking a plum from the Jew's box, to Drabik* And now tell us what's behind all these activities in Bohemia. A Lutheran, aren't you?

DRABIK *bursts out laughing* Lord, you make us laugh with your Luther! The German lords invented him in order to keep Peter's pence in the country. Luther in German is just the same as a priest in Roman. Luther's reply to the articles of the peasants' uprising, when they refused to starve any longer, was to invite the princes "to stab and strangle as much as they could." His peace was for the princes "to strike down the rebellious peasants like mad dogs." There is no difference between him and your jesuitical soul.

EMPEROR *covering his face with his hands as if he were covering up his thoughts; disguising his voice* You know that the Jesuits have been expelled from the country. Whoever has sent you, ventriloquist, you thief of souls, going round Vienna spreading the new spirit, tell us, in one word, what is needful. You can speak openly. We will not take a free word ill. We give you Our word as a nobleman.

DRABIK *taking the Bible out of his pocket* My lord Emperor, the Bohemians can read in their language just as well as Your Grace can in your Latin. Since when has God abolished his commandment, "Thou shalt not kill"? *shouting* Give the people peace! *turning to face the crowd of onlookers, who join in the cry*

CROWD *rebelliously* Peace!

MONK *the showman runs into his arms and he grabs him by the collar; speaking in gloomy tones to the people, who look horrified as they listen* Adamites they are that hold their women in common. They threw crucifixes, holy pictures and prayer books on the dung-cart, emptied their bladders over them and called it a new baptism. They throw Christ out of their homes, crying out that it is the wrong Christ, the nobles have stolen the right one from them. They want to abolish private property, they call that communism and claim it's in the Bible. Did not Pope Urban renew the Bull of the Lord's Supper, the *Coena Domini*, in which heretics, Hussites and Wycliffites are damned? This horde, that both defiles the churches and breaks up the temporal order, must be utterly destroyed. *softly to Ferdinand* There is great danger in this new spirit, that appears in the streets as public opinion and stirs up the people with pamphlets and newspapers, even greater danger than in all the diplomatic intrigues and coalitions the powers have set in motion against the Empire.

FERDINAND *to the monk* Providence is with Us.

MONK *not releasing the half-dead showman; he has both hands clamped round his neck* How long will the Trinity, that is so visibly with Your Highness, tolerate a German Emperor who is a mere human being, afflicted with tolerance and weaknesses.

FERDINAND *imperiously* Who gives orders here apart from Ourselves? Let the fellow go, monk!

DRABIK *half strangled at the hands of the fanatical monk, recovers consciousness and takes out of his jerkin a Bible with the Utraquist symbol of the chalice on its title page* Deus libera me quem diabolus volebat strangulare.

FERDINAND *staring into space; his mouth grows cruel, he has come to a decision; to the Jew* Loyola's order could stand surety in Bohemia for the guarantees which your co-religionists in Paris and London are demanding. Bohemia is rich in gold and silver, if only the miners would dig hard enough. Reading, writing and arithmetic can be learnt from the Jesuits as well. People in Vienna are trying to persuade us to send the Jesuits away for the sake of peace. Very well, let's send them to Bohemia. *rubbing his hands with a gloating smile* They must find this teacher who washes their brains in Bohemia. That would be the way of putting rebellious reason to the service of the state. *turning abruptly to the monk, menacingly* Who is the teacher there who teaches them to read and write? Put the heretic to the question, and may Heaven have mercy on his soul!

SCENE THREE

The throne room in the Amalienburg in Vienna. The Empress Elizabeth stands in the doorway of the ante-room; she has a crown in her black hair, a scarlet velvet Spanish ceremonial dress covered in pearls; childish but cunning, excessively pious and inscrutable, a great beauty; beside her the monk, Valerianus.

MONK *softly to the Empress* . . . and remind His Highness, your husband, how Habsburg, always in loyal devotion to the popes, united with Spain to spread its rule over an immense empire, so that within its bounds the sun never set . . .

EMPRESS *seeing the Emperor in the throne room talking to the Jew* The man in the Emperor is not yet quite dead. He gives me looks. *angrily* The Emperor is spending too long in discussion! *stamps her foot, about to turn away, shaking her fist at the Emperor* He . . . he . . . an animal suffers if it has to stand, thirsting, in the sun, how much more a human being! Monk, you are more than my father, my father confessor!

MONK *pointing to a prayer-stool with a picture of the Virgin hanging above it* Pray, pray when it concerns matters beyond earthly reason. My child!

EMPRESS *fervently* To the Sorrowful Mother of the Redeemer!
The following exchanges simultaneously with the foregoing:

EMPEROR *in conversation with the Jew* . . . two hundred and forty million imperial thalers Wallenstein's demanding to bring peace to the Empire . . . Our word as Emperor on it, it is the last war, the war to put an end to war.

SHYLOCK . . . the war to subdue rebellious reason . . . *wrings his hands.*

EMPEROR *to the Jew, anxiously* Collect money from your co-religionists at the exchanges in London and Paris, and your people will be tolerated in the empire, I give you my word as Emperor. You We raise to the rank of imperial baron!

SHYLOCK *moved* On the other hand, if the Jew does not cheat the people and screw exorbitant interest out of them at the ruler's command, he can expect a pogrom. *aside* General Wallenstein is prepared to fight for the one true faith, but he must have money, that I know from a reliable source. *thinking, making calculations on a sheet of paper* And what security can Your Majesty offer the foreign bankers?

EMPEROR *with satisfaction* Bohemia is overflowing with milk and honey like your Promised Land. Your demands will be in the safe keeping of the Holy Office. Your people will be under the protection of the Emperor.

SHYLOCK *shrugging his shoulders* Truly, you know how to drive a tough bargain, my lord Emperor, but a Yid's still a Yid, even if he becomes the emperor's official Yid. So be it! *he signs a financial document for the Emperor* We're an odd trinity on Christendom's ship of fools. Reasons of State, common sense . . .

EMPEROR *with a laugh* Ha, ha, books burn better than heretics, and don't leave a nasty smell . . .

SHYLOCK *as he goes off* . . . and the Yid as the guilty conscience of the Holy Roman Empire.

PRIVY COUNSELORS *rushing into the throne room* Your Majesty, under torture the Bohemian showman has confessed that the Prague rabble has thrown Lord Slavata, Lord Martinetz and the Imperial Secretary Fabrizius out of the window of Hradcany Castle when they were going to read out the Imperial proclamation. Unrest in Bohemia, Your Majesty! Rebellion!

EMPEROR *impatiently* And who is the man who is proclaiming the new gospel in our Bohemia?

PRIVY COUNSELORS He said he did not know, said he had only learnt it through the newspapers.

EMPEROR *horrified* The throne is tottering, and therefore the Holy See too!

MONK *to the Empress, shouting, with burning eyes* A miracle from the Mother of God, who sent us the heretic at the last moment! Otherwise the Emperor's forbearance would have lost not only Bohemia for Rome, but the whole Empire. *to the Emperor* May the soul of the poor sinner rest in eternal peace, it is in the cause of peace we are sacrificing him! The showman is being led to the stake even now.

EMPEROR *gloating, after one of his counselors whispered something in his ear* One miracle after another! The Queen of Heaven ensured the lords were unharmed by their fall from the window. We have just been informed that they fell onto the dung heap. *with an indifferent glance at the pile of faggots round the stake, amused applause among the kneeling privy counselors. Guards enter, lackeys, heralds with the Imperial standards, knights, magnates, clergy, officers in uniform. The curtains before the throne open, chamberlains dress the Emperor: a gleaming breastplate on which the sun gleams, the Imperial Sword, the Orb. The Emperor leads the Empress to the throne, impatiently snatches the crown out of the Monk's hands and places it — askew — on his own head. He sits beside the Empress.*
In barking tones We have resolved to call this Imperial Diet so that the things We have decreed should be heard and obeyed by Our knights and noble lords! Our late cousin promised a general amnesty. We, Ferdinand, by God's grace his successor on the throne, are minded to keep an imperial word. We intended to carry out the Edict of Forgiveness, in which We had promised to allow those of a different faith to leave the country. It is truly said that man has but a short life, so there is nothing We can do here on earth more consistent with reason than to keep Ourselves in readiness. . . for Heaven! We thank the Jesuits for the art of interpreting the Word in its double meaning, and have therefore decided to send the heretics to our Lord God. May he be a lenient judge for these defiant

subjects! After the pomp and circumstance of this prologue, that has united the court and the people, We intend to enter into serious discussions as to how the Empire should be reconstituted. It is Our desire to rule from Our Imperial chancelleries over an empire of peace. We have in mind the spiritual welfare of the peoples with which we are enlarging the Empire. From Naples to the Skagerrak and beyond the ocean will its western provinces stretch, its eastern bounds beyond Poland's forests to the Orient. But henceforth no pronouncements are to be made about the rights of the individual nations, for absolute sovereignty belongs to the Emperor alone. One *Reich*, one Lord, one Lord God! A world at peace!

BOHEMIAN KNIGHT *interrupting* Sire, the title of ruler of the Holy Roman Empire is not some magic formula which turns any usurpation of rights into a legal act! In Bohemia Your Majesty would be accused of dangerous attacks on the nation's freedom if the people had to drop everything and do what the Emperor ordered. Our people can read and write! In Bohemia we respect liberties, they are guaranteed and sealed in our rights.

EMPEROR *fanatically* Beware, sir knight! We would rather the breastplate on Our body were hacked to pieces, than that We should tolerate a rejection from that heretical land that has been a disturber of the peace of Europe for a thousand years, and whose people, foreign to us in its origins, came from the barbaric east. You Bohemian lords, if you refuse to abandon your sectarian ideas, will be beheaded. In order to secure peace in the Empire, the Emperor has the right not only to goods and possessions, but above all to souls. Humbly do We thank Providence for giving us the power to avert this danger to the freedom of Christianity in the Empire for all time. A legitimate Providence inspires Us to lay down what Our much-loved subjects are to understand by freedom in future. Since We are the fount of justice, We would, were We to do otherwise, sin against Providence, which by mysterious means has brought Us out of the darkness to unite the world.

SEVERAL BOHEMIAN KNIGHTS We are content to let this list of the victories, which our ancestors won for the House of Habsburg, speak for us.

EMPEROR *knocks the list out of the Knights' hands with his scepter* Lest a madman lay hands on the wealth of Bohemia in order to venture an attack on Our Imperial peace, our Holy Inquisition is to seek out the bands of heretics in their remotest hiding places, smoke them out of their mountain caves along with their spawn. All their worldly goods shall be forfeit! An example must be made to put the human race in fear and trembling for all time. Pray God to enlighten you, my Bohemian lords, before God's Steward dictates what is right to your whining and pleading delegations with the sharp blade of the sword. We alone have the power to command, We, the Emperor of the Holy Roman Empire of the German Nation. "Whose the region, his the religion." Monk, we appoint you Grand Inquisitor of the ecclesiastical tribunal in Prague. On Our own authority, We tear up this scrap of paper, the edict of Our predecessor which promised freedom of conscience in all the territories of the Empire, even in those newly conquered by the Imperial army or newly incorporated by treaty. With impatience We await the news of the acceptance of Our new decree by the estates in Bohemia and Moravia, to which the secret couriers of Our chancellery were dispatched weeks ago. *to the counselors* Imperial counselors, hear Our will! We have resolved to make an example and chop off the heads of the City Council of Prague. I want them set up, as an example, on the bridge tower of Charles Bridge, some facing the New Town, others the Lesser Town. Those whose lives We spare because they have repented their obstinacy, shall, insofar as they are state servants, merely have their right hands removed; the others, whose guilt is less, shall have their tongues slit and then be imprisoned or expelled from the country. The German nobles who have stood by the true faith are to divide up their property among them. *The German nobles rattle their weapons in acceptance, the Bohemians shout in protest.*

BOHEMIAN LORDS *furious* A unified German Empire means unified slavery!

EMPEROR Guards! Take these Bohemian lords out and count their heads for me. Deal with the latter as ordered. We prefer a devastated to a heretical Bohemia, if that nation resists the Christian order of the Empire.

GUARDS *carry out the order*

COLONEL GORDON *brutally* Four hundred and ten heads, Your Majesty. Antinomianists the lot! *they are led away* The only business the Imperial Army has in its blood and bones is hanging and beheading. *aside* In Scotland I have seen many warriors with the Bible in their hand opening their mouths wide for their faith; the first time was always their last.

EMPEROR Our tried and trusted Colonel Gordon will requisition sufficient funds from the Imperial war-chest to buy soldiers.

COLONEL GORDON *aside* Starvation is a hereditary disease in the German Empire. The German princes have always been Mars' cheapest recruiting agents.

EMPEROR Nobles, you are dismissed; go to join the army. Our loyal Field Marshal Lord Wallenstein is to take command of the Imperial forces.

WALLENSTEIN *steps forward, bows and takes the baton; the gathering departs, apart from Wallenstein and his wife*

EMPEROR *creeps quietly to the balcony, opens the doors; looking out into the smoke-covered park* Air! Air! The pain in my entrails is agonizing. Had I not had some more of those Carlsbad plums, I would be suffering almost as much as our Bohemian brother, the showman, who will soon be fanning himself in paradise.

WALLENSTEIN *thoughtfully watching the Emperor on the balcony; his wife comes to him* Is it really the Emperor's will that the Spanish Inquisition should operate in my country with fire and sword? I'm getting old, Katharina, I can feel it in my bones.

HIS WIFE *sitting down in an alcove* Husband dear, I feel weak from all this standing, carrying your child in my belly as I am. And you are going to go off to war again? Will there never come a time when men will sit round a table, conferring, instead of standing round like iron skeletons? How can I embrace you, husband, my frailty-in-armor, who pretend to be the roller that will set the ship of state afloat again! *jumping up to embrace him* As if a woman could ever clasp the full measure of her love in her arms. My heart trembles for your life, husband.

WALLENSTEIN Why do women not wear a breastplate over their hearts?

HIS WIFE That would kill the children that she bears in her womb for nine months.

WALLENSTEIN When a woman is about to become a mother, truly, she feels more loving-kindness in her breast than all the gods, for whom men kill each other. *looking round warily, his finger to his lips* Could Comenius have been right after all to teach the brethren in Bohemia to read the Gospel of peace?

EMPEROR *on the balcony, without irony, without conviction, shivering in his furs, even though the spring sun is shining; looking at the Empress* Beautiful she is, my Italian, standing there timidly by the door. *to her, affably, exhilarated* Empress, let us see how, instead of the Moor, the first heretic from Bohemia burns.
Through the balcony door the park and woods can be seen, but also the square below the castle. The Empress kisses the Emperor's hand. Silence. From the park comes the sound of the people shouting, processions of monks and nuns can be seen

streaming into the park and taking up their places; the park is full of emblems of the cross.

1st VOICE FROM THE PEOPLE But it was the Jews and not the Protestants who nailed the Savior to the cross!

2nd VOICE FROM THE PEOPLE The Jews drain the blood from innocent children. Why does the Emperor protect them?

3rd VOICE FROM THE PEOPLE They have to mix it into their Easter bread, the sons of Belial, to get rid of the noxious smell, because they go to court!

4th VOICE FROM THE PEOPLE They cheat good Christian folk and extort interest from them, all for the sake of money. Have mercy on the Bohemian Brother, he's a man like us . . .

5th VOICE FROM THE PEOPLE The whole world will be subject to the Elders of Zion, even the Holy Roman Emperor in Vienna. In their souls, the good-hearted folk of Vienna will not suffer it to happen. *The sentence is read out. Horses paw the ground, the preparations of the executioners' henchmen can be heard; a column of smoke rises; cries of terror from Drabik, who is being led to the stake; the crowd becomes aroused like wild animals before feeding; altar bells are rung; the cries of pain are drowned by outbreaks of delight among the crowd when they see the condemned man wearing the heretic's cap.*

EMPRESS *takes out her handkerchief*

EMPEROR *softening* Eleonore, do you feel ill? I'll pardon the poor devil. *to the secretary* The bonfire is to be put out. The man is pardoned.
The order is carried out. The mob breaks out into cries of fury, would have torn the man from the hands of the guards, had they fallen back.

EMPRESS *nods* Is that enough? Enough? If it were an infidel Moor, as in Spain . . . but to burn a Christian . . .

EMPEROR You shouldn't be so old-fashioned, Eleonore! We are living in a new age, an age of tolerance. Nowadays we prefer to ship the blacks out to the plantations in the New World. That brings in money which we badly need. I have an idea. Instead of executing the agitator here, I'll simply make a present of him to the city of Calvin. They'll make things hot for him there, just as they did for that freethinker from Charles the Fifth's entourage. Wasn't it through Calvin's burning of Servetus, after he had fled to Geneva, that the Reformation showed its true face?
Emperor and Empress exit

ACT TWO

SCENE ONE

Fulnek, a town on the border between Moravia and Silesia; 1628, early spring. By the river, stalls on the bank, a castle in the background. In and outside the candlemaker's shop.

CANDLEMAKER *arguing with some men who have come out of the woods with honeycombs from the wild bees, which they are selling to him*

WOOD-FOLK There's something wrong with your weights! For the same amount of wax as we brought last year we get half portions?

CANDLEMAKER *blowing the flame under his pot with the bellows* The country's at war. We all have to get used to changes. Pack up that millet and that fat bacon before I change my mind. *to his assistants* Put on some dry pine-logs, lads, with lots of resin, we need to get the wax soft enough for candles quicker this time. *to the wood-folk, who are packing the food they have exchanged for the wax away in their haversacks* What do you savages expect, anyway, all you can do is raid bees' nests. What do you know about our craft, anyway? It's no goldmine any longer since the soap-boilers started muscling in on our business, and we get cutthroat competition from the butchers, they're the worst, making their farthing dips from tallow. That's progress for you!

1st OF THE WOOD-FOLK *still angry* Things are getting better and better for you since you've become an elder of the Brethren and joined the Protestants . . . you own a house, a business . . . and you're a town councillor.

CANDLEMAKER And the Swedes'll pay our outstanding bills, eh?

Comenius 197

1st OF THE WOOD-FOLK The materials are piled up in your shed by the hundredweight ready for the funeral candles every household will soon be ordering when war comes . . .

CANDLEMAKER *whining* . . . on credit! War's the time for debtors and thieves. Just listen and I'll tell you why I went over to the Anabaptists that time. In those days, who was buying Christmas cribs with little wax figures, or votive offerings — wax hands and feet, bridal candles, the infant Jesus in swaddling clothes, candles for pilgrimages — to call the saints' intercession down from heaven to ward off illness from themselves or their family, to protect their cattle and their barns? But since everyone in Bohemia has started protesting against the divine order of things, in which everything was arranged for the best, Czechs as well as Germans . . . *sighs, clasps his fat hands over his belly* We're not allowed to speak! *drinks mead, fortified* Are you going to let me have the wax at that price or not? Wax is getting too dear anyway. I'm thinking of switching to hops instead. I can brew mead just as well as Lopatsky next door, he's going over to beer entirely, genuine Czech beer for the Emperor's soldiers, and with an indulgence from the bishop. *pays off the wood-folk* There you are! And I'll put in an extra King Wenceslas thaler, there's still silver from the old days in that! Maybe I'll soon be needing wax for altar candles if peace breaks out and they say all those masses. We sweat and slave for our wives and the little ones. Here. Drink a health to the country, and let's hope the war doesn't last too long. *puts out beakers for them and fills them with mead. The wood-folk grin to themselves, wipe their hands over their beards, and start to stare out of the window, at the same time talking and laughing*

SCENE TWO

Outside the shop. Amos Comenius joins them: red hair, black clothes; with him his little adopted daughter, who is blind.

COMENIUS Get me another wax candle, will you, candlemaker. This very night I'm going to start writing my *Didactica Magna*. The aim of the book is to tell the little ones, the simple in spirit, about all things found in nature, and to teach them to understand habits and customs, so that they will love one another. A humane nursery school for all peoples, as long as they are children, as long as their hearts are malleable and their spirits young, so they can understand that the world can be a paradise, instead of the labyrinth in which we have trapped ourselves.

CANDLEMAKER *more interested in the procession* War's coming and you want children to go to school? The time's not ripe!

COMENIUS *with the greatest calm in the world* Keep your war-cries to yourself, candlemaker, otherwise you will make me angry at such lack of reason.

CANDLEMAKER *stroking Christl's head* Is this your child?

COMENIUS No, a foster child. She's blind.

CANDLEMAKER *with an exaggerated sigh* There's a lot of misery in the world, and soon there'll be more for the poor. Well then, my little fever-brow, you'll have to get the Pastor to tell you what there is to be seen all around. Is the child Czech?
Shouts. Girls in blue dresses open the procession. Like the rest, they have lighted candles on their heads.

CANDLEMAKER *out loud* My children are healthy and chubby, thank God, all three of them girls, those in blue at the front, do you see them, wood-folk?

WOOD-FOLK . . . and the biggest candles towering atop their hollow pumpkins, the candlemaker's three always at the front!

CHRISTL Tell me, father, what kind of clothes do the village children have on? Are they still a long way from the river? Is big Jaromir leading the dance again? Did you teach them the poem they're singing?

COMENIUS So many questions at once, I'll have to make my eyes dart here and there, like birds snapping everything up before it's past them. *piercing cries of joy from the children* At the front of the procession is big Jaromir, who lisps because he has a gap in his teeth, he's leading the way on stilts, making funny gestures with his arms. Give me your arms and I'll show you. And now there's a wild gang of boys, jumping over the ice-floes, waving sticks and chasing the girls, who are behaving themselves and following the procession. The boys are trying to put their candles out. On the ends of their sticks they have hens' eggs they've blown and tied to ribbons with colors that glow like fire. Some of the eggs are well-aimed and put the candles out, but the girls light them again from the girl's beside them. Now the girls are clapping their hands, the bigger girls with the candles are forming a circle, the little ones are gathered round a straw doll, busying themselves dressing it. Vlasta's lending it her kerchief, Anushka her jacket and Jana her neatly pleated ruff. They're lifting the doll they've dressed up onto a wooden frame, and now they'll go over the bank and down to the river, where we can't see them any more. There they're going to throw the doll into the river, in its old clothes it represents winter. Now listen to what they're singing, how well the river throws the words back to you. The hollow eggs are floating down the river with little candles burning inside them. It's spring!

CHILDREN *singing*
. . . we carry the winter out of the farm
and bring a new year back in . . .
shouting, then singing again
Winter dark, winter cold
float away down the stream.
Boys and girls all come and eat

crimson eggs and yellow cakes.
The stamping of a round-dance can be heard.

GIRLS Sun, sun, where've you been all this time?

BOYS At the well, in the water, in the sea.

GIRLS Violet and rose cannot bloom
unless the sun shines peace upon us.

BOYS Hey, Saint Peter in Rome,
stand us a bottle of mead
so we can quench our thirst.
During the last two verses the children come to collect money from the candlemaker, Christl too gets a copper for herself from Comenius, and they buy gingerbread. Beside themselves with joy, they surround Comenius, who has to sit down on the doorstep, while Christl makes room for a small child on the teacher's knee.

COMENIUS Off you go, children, your parents will be waiting, it's getting dark.

CHILDREN We made the ceremony for us children, we're playing Welcome to Spring. Tell us a story before we let you go!

ALL Yes, a story!

COMENIUS *looking at the candlemaker's sign, which represents a beehive* Right, children, just to give your feverish brows a chance to cool down. The candlemaker's shop-sign suggests a tale to me. There was once a time when our nation was like the bees, when our land was still one vast forest. The rime never melted and the frost never thawed, never sparkled like dew. The Czechs were like guests who had woken too early, before the rest of the house was up. And they lived in the woods, wearing the skins of wild animals, that was the way people in the country dressed in those days. Only Libussa went out in a dress made of linen she had woven herself and embroidered with colored thread. At each step she took she felt as if a bird were calling out to her: Already awake, Libussa?

Because Libussa was a sorceress, she only had to look in the little mirror she carried in her pocket — just as you girls look at pictures in a book of fairy tales — to see the Queen Bee going for a ride in her coach. Libussa stood aside to let it pass, and the Queen Bee bowed to her and asked her to get into the coach. "You're up first, Miss Libussa, so early in the morning!" Libussa was shy of imposing on her, so she simply asked for advice on how to found a state for the Czechs in Bohemia. That very morning the Queen Bee explained how to go about it, until they both had to part, because of breakfast — naturally Miss Libussa couldn't take her coffee cup with her to the beehive. And that's why she wasn't wide enough awake to remember the Queen Bee's instructions exactly.

After Libussa, following the bee's instructions, had founded her state run by the girls, there was a lot of shouting to be heard out in the fields. Two farmers were arguing about a boundary marker. In their furs they looked like bears, and they were waving their heavy cudgels at each other. They saw Miss Libussa and they said to themselves, open-mouthed, "Doubtless she must be some highly respected doctor," and they asked her to settle their argument. Desperately Libussa racked her brains to remember how the Queen Bee would have settled such an argument. And her white unicorn, which would also have given her good advice, she had sent out to graze in the forest. At a complete loss, she kept looking from one of the farmers to the other. The one had a shock of red hair, but the other had blue eyes and slim hips. Eventually she gave her verdict in favor of the one who was less well-favored, everyone knows that red hair brings misfortune. She gave him a kiss, slyly asking the other whether it was going to rain, to make him look up at the sky. She bit her red lips because the one with such innocent eyes and slim hips and blond hair, Premisl by name, instead of courting her, started grumbling angrily. He made her stammer with his questions, "Who are you anyway? Why are you interfering here? No one asked you." The men decided to choose a prince. During the election she was, as the chronicle says, "supported on cushions." The men's decision probably caused her much pain. The burgomasters conducted the elections in the field. Without a parasol Libussa had to follow the farmer's plow, and gather the sheaves of Premisl, who had been elected the queen's husband and Prince of Bohemia. Libussa's eyes filled with tears, for Premisl had more important things to do. That very same day he wanted to plow up enough land to build a capital on for his Bohemian kingdom. Since those days it has been men who have ruled here, but peace has grown rare. *stands up, they all shout and laugh*

WOOD-FOLK *as they leave* You told your story well, teacher. You spoke well about the bees, better than we can, and we're the ones who know about them. If Wallenstein should come to Fulnek, then our fists will remain your friends. Although we are German, you can count on us when danger threatens. One, two, three, hup! Everyone got his ax? *shouldering their tools and sacks, they leave.*

COMENIUS Unfortunately, good folk like that only grow in the woods, not in the cities.*off*

SCENE THREE

Fulnek Castle, spring. In one corner an oak in full leaf under which stands Comenius, who is just sending the children home. On the ground a globe, he has been teaching them about the shape of the earth. Zerotin's wife still on horseback, her host, Baron Skrbensky, has already dismounted on the other side of the stage.

SKRBENSKY My lady, you have a fine mount, you set a sharp pace. How did you like seeing the country again?

ZEROTIN'S WIFE It was a splendid ride. I give you heartfelt thanks for the excursion, Baron Skrbensky. Truly, your castle lies in enchanting countryside, from the wooded hills the fresh air carries the balm of the evergreen pines right into its chambers. I remember how — it is almost a year ago now — staying here cured me when I was in a despondent humor. Only nature can soothe the pain that each one of us must feel, now that war and all its misfortunes threaten. *becoming impatient* There is a splendid smell of roast meat from the kitchens. Tell the ladies the meal is served.

ZEROTIN *coming through the gate* At last, my wife!

Skrbensky goes into the castle; other knights come through the gate and gather round the lady on horseback, she examines the group, looking for someone.

ZEROTIN We were already worried you might be lost, dear friend. It was Skrbensky who found you?

ZEROTIN'S WIFE *in a cool conversational tone to the group*
I saw something very rare. Two eagles were fighting, almost right over my head, so close I could hear the flap of their wings, see the foliage, touched by their wing-beats, quiver in the tree-tops.

ZEROTIN Are you not going to dismount?
The nobles give the beautiful lady admiring glances, each wants to assist her, she points to Trcka. With an unconscious, hesitant gesture, she hands the reins to Trcka.

ZEROTIN'S WIFE *in a conversational tone* Baron Trcka, I recognize you. This chance meeting means I can show you my favorite horse. I never let anyone else ride it, and when it grows old I will never mount another. *jumps down, holds out her hand to him, which he kisses; to her husband* Tell them to give the stallion its oats!
She becomes impatient; the group leaves; a servant takes the horse. Zerotin turns to Comenius and goes center stage with him, looking at a book.

ZEROTIN'S WIFE *to Trcka* At last they've gone! I hoped I might see you while I was out riding?

TRCKA *softly* You've come!

ZEROTIN'S WIFE *softly* The separation was so long I couldn't bear it any more. Did I not promise you I would come to Fulnek this summer? *can hardly control herself with happiness*

TRCKA Be more careful, my darling!

ZEROTIN'S WIFE If only all my plans would succeed so well, my love. If only it were soon night! *unrestrained* If I hadn't spoken to you right away, I would have been so impatient I would have started to think we would never be together again. How can I find my way through these our new times? Tell me, will there be even more happiness, more love in the future?

TRCKA What a woman you are! But here comes your husband. He's always with that schoolmaster instead of on our side. Unlike a woman, a man has to be able to make a decision, to be positive. Emperor, pope, duke and rich man, or monk and poor man, beggar-man, thief: as long as men rule the world, that is the divine order, each man in his proper station. All these radical teachings of the Unity of Brethren do nothing to stop the rebel hordes from smashing the stained-glass windows in the cathedrals and the statues on tombs, burning rare and sacred books, scratching off murals depicting our traditional spiritual values and behavior. No; a mortar discharged into the middle of the rebel troops and guarantees for our privileges would be preferable to the pastor's new ideas, to all this sentimental twaddle about the poverty and misery of the little man.

ZEROTIN'S WIFE In all your politics, do not forget us women, my proud lord. A poor woman bore the Son of Man, our Redeemer from all earthly sorrows. *faster and more urgently* Will nothing ever come between our love? If you had only seen the pair of loving eagles, magnificent creatures, symbols of our undying love. I have done everything for you, dearest, I am expecting a child.

ZEROTIN *approaches with Comenius; introducing him* The pastor of our Unity of Brethren, my spiritual brother, has dedicated a book to me . . .

ZEROTIN'S WIFE *with a cursory glance* Let me see the title, pastor.

COMENIUS My lady, my book is called "The Labyrinth of the World" . . .

ZEROTIN'S WIFE *uninterested* An edifying work, I presume?

COMENIUS *admonishing tone* . . . to find calm in the harbor of our conscience, for it is as if we were at sea with a storm threatening.

TRCKA *ironically* . . . before lightning strikes! *aside to Zerotin's wife* . . . I have to stop the pastor delivering his sermon on mystical love. I prefer a drink with the others. *aloud* Enjoy yourselves. *leaving, aside* The pastor is still around, even though he has been proscribed.

COMENIUS *urgently to Zerotin's wife* I wrote this book instead of a "Via Lucis," that I must put off until more peaceful times, because of the blow from Vienna that struck our community. Since all security has vanished from under our feet, the brethren have asked me for guidance to accompany them on their journeyings as exiles who must bid farewell to their homeland. And since, until now, the weal and woe of our community depended on you Zerotin, our venerable noble lord and brother, I have dedicated this simple record of my thoughts to you and your revered wife. My book is neither a romantic, metaphysical renunciation of the world, nor an exciting novel, as is usual nowadays, but a description of the labyrinth of the world, as it appears to our senses, in which the human race, although endowed with reason and an immortal soul, has lost its way. We come into the world, as into a ballroom of pleasures and desires, with a mask over our face. The old Greeks told of a labyrinth in which youths and maidens were sacrificed to a monster, until a hero took pity on them. For us, who live under northern skies, salvation can no longer be expressed in such ancient symbols. "Melancholy," that is what Master Dürer wrote on his engraved drawing of the man of our time. Thus we are: alone, and all our reason leaves us no hope, since we lost the paradise of our heart. Force compels us, the Brethren, to bid you farewell, noble lord.

ZEROTIN Stay with us, father! Will the shepherd leave his flock?

SCENE FOUR

Hall in Fulnek Castle, evening gathering of lords and ladies.
TRCKA *with biting scorn* Ladies and gentlemen, do you realize you have just six months to accept the religion of the Empire?

MORAVIAN NOBLEMAN But at his coronation for the crownlands of Bohemia and Moravia the new emperor swore a special oath to uphold his late uncle's edict of tolerance . . .

ZEROTIN . . . and put his signature below that of the late Emperor Matthias and appended his seal.

BOHEMIAN LORD *rebelliously* In Prague we have been forbidden to summon the diets. One decree follows on the heels of the last, already the imperial troops are burning and pillaging because we flung Slavata, Martinetz, and their secretary out of the window of Hradcany Castle. The persecution is most vigorous in Bohemia because nowhere else has the Reformation taken such deep root, among the nobles as well as the common people. We set up a provisional government . . .

TRCKA *interrupting* The Moravian Brethren cannot follow your example, your provisional government is without a head since the Battle of the White Mountain, and your Winter King has fled to England.

BOHEMIAN LORD The Count Palatine has not yet given up our righteous cause, his wife will bring us England's aid. By the Bible I swear one should obey God, and not Caesar.

TRCKA *in response* How much value can one put on a Bohemian Bible? You have to use common sense. England is a far-away country, while one could still negotiate with the nobles. But did this rabble of Taborites and Hussites keep their hands off our privileges? What use will all Pastor Comenius' ideas on peace be to us lords if lawlessness, anarchy and a refusal to pay taxes prevail?

ZEROTIN *timidly* But, my noble lords, do you not agree with the opinion of the godly that there has been enough bloodshed in all countries? Out pastor Comenius teaches us, "Thou shalt not kill." And that means that even the Emperor does not have the right to turn the commandment on its head, whether for Catholics or Protestants.

BOHEMIAN LORD *bitterly* . . . even the Pope follows the heathen dictum, "Si vis pacem, para bellum."

TRCKA *forcefully to Zerotin's wife* When will you get round to telling your husband he must send the preacher packing if he wants to preserve his own freedom!?

A MORAVIAN BARON *to Trcka scornfully* As I heard Cardinal Caspar say on the occasion of the banquet for the coronation in Prague, even the Church does not have the right to issue an absolute veto against all kinds of war. On the contrary, the Curia in Rome sees even a war of aggression as justified, as long as it is waged in order to right a wrong after other means have failed.

BOHEMIAN NOBLE Our intention is to defend our national rights. How would it be if we were to vote to see who supports his country's cause? In Prague we already have our martyrs, the twenty-seven noblemen who suffered for the cause of the Bohemian nation. We will arm the people! Away with the imperial eagle, let the Bohemian lion be our standard.

ZEROTIN *composed* I am, and shall remain, the Emperor's vassal.

ZEROTIN'S WIFE *in a firm tone to him, quietly, aside* The Emperor will negotiate, just as Matthias did. I wish you would not insist on discussing all these matters, which are quite straightforward, with that preacher who has been proscribed. Instead, you should follow the advice of your fellow nobles. No nation which plans for more coffins than cradles will achieve sovereignty. You must hear what my brother Wallenstein writes from the imperial headquarters in Eger. Baron Trcka, read out your letter.

TRCKA *jumps up onto the table and reads the letter out loud* All noble lords who grant asylum to anyone who has been proscribed can expect the full rigor of the law. From now on no follower of this sect, who call themselves the Godly Brethren and who preach the overthrow of the prevailing order, shall be allowed to remain in our crownlands of Bohemia and Moravia. Our patrols will seek them out and hunt them down in the other lands of our crown, where secret agreements have been made to deliver these traitors up to our officials. Given in the imperial chancellery, this day of . . .
to all in a loud voice We must deliver up Pastor Comenius or we will all have to pay for it.

ZEROTIN *in despair, to his wife* Sacrifice Comenius? What will people think of me afterward? Even these knights, whose gambling and womanizing and quick familiarity disgust me, would think it improper of me to betray my friend. At the gaming table they wager their faith as well as their fortune on a throw of the dice.

TRCKA *trying to draw Zerotin out of the group of knights* My friend, you seem to have forgotten the taste of the blood of the vines that our great king from the House of Luxemburg planted at Melnik. *pours out a goblet of red wine and forces Zerotin to empty it; turns to the assembled company, in a merry mood* Who would have expected to see our godly Zerotin drinking!

ZEROTIN *tries, furiously but in vain, to defend himself* What? Betray the voice of reason? Lose my way in the labyrinth of the world? Betray my friend and my Emperor too.
Shrill whistles are heard; the knights, who are somewhat tipsy, suddenly start in fright and leap up.

KNIGHTS The imperial army in Fulnek already?

TRCKA *in reassuring tones* You're seeing double, my friends, and your bad consciences too. Let us be merry men at the gaming table, let us throw the dice for fame, power and the favor of Dame Fortune, like Wallenstein, who is standing at the gate of Fulnek, ready to climb to the top, step by step. No Emperor will follow him up there, once he has reached the summit of the Bohemian-Moravian Empire.

ZEROTIN *watches, apparently absentminded, as his wife goes up to Trcka*

TRCKA Please, Countess, compose yourself. We'll dance. *from the neighboring room comes the sound of a fiddle playing a peasant dance*

ZEROTIN'S WIFE *to Trcka, whispering* I have done everything for you, everything. Are you content? My brother is at the door, Wallenstein is going to drop his mask. *out loud* Let us dance! *softly* I am going mad with longing. Let us dance.

TRCKA *louder* This is a step I do not know. Let us go over there, by the wall, and practice it together. Otherwise I will tread on your toes, and I would suffer for it. *turning to the company, even louder* The tune is new to me. Does it come from Bohemia? *to Zerotin's wife* Don't hold me so close, you'll give us away. Listen, tonight, as soon as dinner is over, I'm going to ride to the imperial headquarters, to your brother, who will put down the Reformation with money from abroad, in order to make himself king. It's not the Emperor, nor the Pope who rules our country in these modern times, it's money.
Wild shouting outside, the doors are broken down with axes and the wood-folk rush in. Trcka frees himself from Zerotin's wife with a kiss, jumps over the table and out through the balcony door.

WOOD-FOLK *go to the balcony and watch him run off; to Zerotin* Where have you locked up our pastor?

ZEROTIN'S WIFE *with a loud cry; the drunken Zerotin has guessed what has passed between his wife and Trcka and is shaking her by the shoulder* He played me false! He has ruined me, body and soul! You men! The beasts of prey are truly your symbols! *immediately pulls herself together and orders the wood-folk to leave* Go! *aside, sobbing* How blind I was, how unsuspecting!

ZEROTIN Woman, what have you done to me? Your forehead covered in sweat, your hair unkempt, and looking as if you had murdered someone . . .

ZEROTIN'S WIFE *has pulled herself together again* . . . or had been murdered. *directly and condescendingly, as if she had put on another mask* If you no longer believe in the pastor, nor in reason, how can I satisfy you, me, a weak woman? *tidying her hair, she retreats step by step as Zerotin follows her*

ZEROTIN . . . never will I be able to lull this moment. His kiss is still burning your lips.

ZEROTIN'S WIFE That was all it needed for you to lose your heart's paradise? *mocking* In spite of all our reason, are we no more than shadows created by our imagination? We simply have to take ourselves as we are, and be nice to one another, since we know better. The audience observing us down there in the stalls is just as much lost in the labyrinth of the world as we are. *both exit*

WOOD-FOLK *in the meantime they have searched all the side-rooms; the guests leave one by one while two of the wood-folk bring Trcka into the banqueting hall from the balcony, tie him to a chair and dress him in a black gown, such as Comenius wears, and put a red wig and beard on him.* You go over there, I'll take the right. We've got our pastor to safety, he's sitting in a pear-tree in the garden until we go to fetch him during the night. That's the way the bees say their farewell to the drones, when there's no longer any room in the hive for them.
The hall empties; silence, then bugle calls, imperial soldiers rush into the hall. It has gone dark.

COLONEL . . . There's still one sitting there. Light! Bring the torches. We've found him, the redbeard, the head of the sect of the godly in this land! We'll get a fine reward for this. Comenius, surrender!

TRCKA *bewildered at this turn of fate; after he has been untied he tears off the red wig, steps out of the black gown, and holds out his hand to the colonel* Colonel! I had as good as set up an ambush for the pastor, but the fox was slyer than I. Here are my papers, Baron Trcka at your service, officer in the imperial guards. Unfortunately the pastor has given us the slip, Colonel. Much to my regret.

COLONEL *saluting* Please excuse me, but it looks as if someone has played a carnival trick on us.

SCENE FIVE

Hungarian border, winter; a tumbledown shack in the mountains; a door to the outside, blowing open and shut in the gale. In the background the deranged Drabik, previously the showman, is fanning an open fire. Comenius is peering out through the door.

DRABIK Still nothing of the exiles to be seen?

COMENIUS The gale is driving the clouds down low and the snowdrifts are obscuring the view of the track. The brethren will not be able to find their way to us up here, not with their heavily laden farm-carts, nor those on foot with their bundles on their backs; they will lose their way in the crags. A bad time for those that cannot find shelter. They are God's creatures just as much as the others sitting in the warmth by their stoves. It is poor comfort that they too will one day have to make their way barefoot to the next world.

DRABIK *worked up* Your dear little Protestant brothers and sisters abroad are averting their eyes from our misery and crossing their hearts and bellies after their own fashion. Pastor, you believe in the great days. And they're coming, on horseback, heels in the stirrups; across the frontier you can see Waldensian brethren, Albigensians, Picards, Cathars, Lombards, all of them Protestants and Communists, peering impatiently at Bohemia because in the past they ate their fill at our conventicles. Where are they? Can you see one single soul? *waving a burning log around violently, he goes to the door, pushes it open* Burning villages down below, not a dog anywhere to be seen.

COMENIUS *leading Drabik back into the hut* The glare from your torch can be seen for miles around, brother, come back in.

DRABIK All the brighter will the torch of Bohemia burn for the whole world to see.

COMENIUS *rejoicing* I can see the first ones coming up round the snowdrift. *opens the door wide. The first refugees enter, dressed in tatters, exhausted. Shrink back in horror when they see Drabik.*

REFUGEES The Devil himself! Keep back, Drabik, showman, are you still alive? A miracle! We heard they had burnt you at the stake in Vienna!

DRABIK *the torch in his hand, in a prophetic pose, which he likes to adopt from time to time* But at the twelfth hour of the night I saw, in the mire of the Flood, face to face, the Emperor with the crown on his head, the great One in the sum of naughts, sitting on his throne of blood, appareled in gold, scepter and orb in his hands. "Have mercy, give me back the breath that slipped out of my entrails on the bonfire," Drabik pleads. And the voice of the Holy Father whispers in the Emperor's ear, "Can a man's breath return like a day that has passed?" And in melancholy tones, the head of the House of Habsburg murmurs, "Acid is the soil in which our roots wither . . ."

BRETHREN *shaking their heads* Many a good Christian's mind has been unhinged. *they settle round the fire*

DRABIK . . . and with ghostly voice, a new spirit, the breath in the dry wood, in my charred body, began to stir, the toad to jump out of the rock. Evil is still attacking good, now good is on top, now evil climbs over it. Since they cannot unite in mating, the one wanting to turn inward, the other outward, mankind began to despair of itself. "See, I am just copying the Father; who made the Father, I don't know." So says Drabik.

AN OLD WOMAN *in a colorful dress and similar headgear, kneeling* Pomiluj ny! You shouldn't take the name of God in vain like our enemies.

ONE OF THE REFUGEES LYING BY THE FIRE *covered with open wounds* Be still, old woman. *to Drabik* Nobody knows who he used to be any more. Help me staunch the blood. The storm in the pines outside seems like a cradle song now, I could sleep for ever. Haven't slept for weeks, with the Emperor's soldiers at our heels. In Trautenau the dragoons herded the godly into the church with bloodhounds and made them recant before a Dominican. But even those who had toed the party line were forced to run, still clutching their absolution, for their farms had been occupied by soldiers; in their cottages with the delicate little pillars the commissar explained to them that in the meantime the Emperor had requisitioned the houses, together with the pretty gables sticking up into the blue sky. *dies*

A YOUNG MAN *angrily* The Elbe bridge collapsed, some of the Brethren fell into the river with their carts. The onlookers used pickaxes to force those who were trying to swim to the bank back into the current. From the opposite bank others shot at the drowning Brethren.

NEWLY ARRIVED REFUGEES *a babble of voices* Peace be with us. We're late because we had to leave the road outside Leitmeritz. Until that far the border police had given us permission to pass. That meant we had to crawl over the ridge, bodies bent forward, the wind was so strong you thought it was going to tear you off your legs. Snow-blind, each holding onto the next in a line, we would have all plunged to our graves if the man at the front had not given a terrible cry as he fell into the abyss. Destitution behind us, destitution before; all men may be equal in Adam, but for us it's no more than skin-deep.

COMENIUS *mildly* Like the Jews, our lot is to be scattered to the four winds. A premonition tells me I will never again tread the ground I come from. I must become a citizen of the world. *sadly takes the Bible and chalice out of his jerkin*

YOUNG MAN *defiantly* Pastor, I come from Prague. Stay with us. We'll return with our Bible and the chalice. *taking a large knife out of his jerkin* We will return, but bearing maces in our mailed fists, like Jan Zizka in the days of old, with his fortresses made of carts drawn up in a circle. You keep the Taborites' Bible and the Hussite chalice you managed to save.

COMENIUS *soothingly* First of all we'll spend the night here, at daybreak we'll be across the frontier, and with the congregation of the Brethren in Poland we'll find refuge from the mercenaries who overran our land.

YOUNG MAN *wildly* In the spirit of the new age we are allied with Luther, who nailed his theses to the church door, with Calvin in Geneva, and Zwingli in Switzerland.

COMENIUS *takes the Bible, looks for a passage, points to it* The new age must not be like the murk, luring us back into a labyrinth, that, like the millennium, we await in the present with bloody deeds. Did Christ not tell Peter to put up his sword? You can all read and write your mother tongue. *holds up the open Bible for all to see* It says here, "Thou shalt not kill." Has God repealed his commandment in this new age?

YOUNG MAN *putting away his knife, discontented* The Antichrist in Rome uses Latin as a means of controlling his flock. Why did we burn the churches and monasteries and libraries, if not to lift the curse that lies on the common man who cannot read?

COMENIUS *still in mild tones* It is my Protestant faith that if mankind is not to sink to an impotent doom, like the prehistoric giants not endowed with reason, Christianity must not be limited to those with a knowledge of a dead or a living language. The Savior is still being crucified, even if the translated Bible can be bought at the fair. Brother! Let us reflect on this freedom in the new spirit of the modern age. The common man can be taught to read and write, but his mind still bears calluses from the past. Are we not all the same, human beings fleeing to a new age, which will not become home to us until people learn reason. Animals can be tamed, shall man alone remain a murderer? *gently, trying to calm the angry lad* You think those are in the right who want to leave young people stuck in their immaturity, all ready to be gobbled up, like sausages dressed in clothes? Do we not take a needle to patch the holes in our clothes so that we do not have to blush for our rags in front of others? Listen, brother, I have been thinking about a plan, about the basis for education. We must start with the little children, in all nations, and teach them to see and understand people and things with open eyes. That, thanks to the creative power of the divinity, unfathomable though it is, is attainable by all mankind. That is my Protestant faith. Then let the dark powers in future try to beat the ass' skin and drum young people into line to get them to kill each other! *laughs out loud*

OLD WOMAN *kneels down and prays*

THE YOUNG MAN *turns toward the door, angrily* Wishful thinking, pastor, your gospel of progress is nothing new. Only the Jesuits use the ancient Latin in order to secure control for the dark powers. Now that lean times have come for them, it's that schoolmaster's pious hope, your school-for-all, that is exploiting the mother tongue because the overworked farmer sleeps through a sermon in Latin. With the laying-on of hands you too, Moderator, soothe the common man into hoisting the bundle willingly onto his back, just so the great lords won't lose their good humor. No! I refuse! Neither priest nor schoolmaster! The common man can find his own way to the table that God has set for all. By nature he has enough brain not to be like the ox and let the rope be strung through his nose. When I hear your bells of peace ringing out against war, then I prefer the wolves to the dogs that hound the game toward the huntsman.

COMENIUS *turning away* In your savagery, you seem to think it a law of nature, settled for all time, that human existence will always resemble the huntsman's craft. *furiously flings open the door*

THE YOUNG MAN It's not only religion you want to reform, you'd like to reform human nature as well; just like the alchemists you want to breed a homunculus in a test-tube. *in the doorway he bumps into de Geert, who is coming in* Here comes the model pupil!

DE GEERT *with a packet of letters, breathlessly* Brother Comenius, I managed to carry these letters unharmed through Bohemia, where I searched for you in vain. Your door opens more quickly than that of the Brethren at home, who fear denunciation and arrest every time someone knocks at the door at night. *reading from the letters* From Poland an invitation to a discussion with Protestant theologians, who cannot come to an agreement about the procedure to be followed at the Lord's supper. An invitation from the parliament in London, whose army is turning against the renegade king. A letter from Cromwell, the Protector, expressing his approval for your idea of a defensive alliance of the Protestant nations, as soon as his army has overcome the Papists. When that is done, he can offer you refuge and subsidies. *continues reading* In this one the Unity of Brethren warns you not to accept the invitation to Poland. Because of your support for the Swedes your former home in Leszno has been reduced to ashes, the Brethren are in flight, your house and library have been burnt to ashes. It is true that the Swedes were victorious against the Papists, but since the death of her father, the great Gustavus Adolphus, who united the Protestant Church, Queen Christina has left Poland to its own devices until the question of the succession is settled peaceably. Oxenstierna, the all-powerful Swedish chancellor, has made peace with the House of Habsburg, and offers you asylum. Tired of the religious quarrels, Queen Christina has, moreover, heard that you recently wrote about your plan for education to the Grand Vizier of Turkey as well, "because according to the Koran all men are equal, and Moses, Jesus and Mohammed are prophets of the God beside whom there is no other god."

COMENIUS *somewhat depressed* The duty to care for mankind has now become more urgent than care for my own fate. Perhaps my belief that God guides human reason is presumptuous? Many consider me a false prophet. Can there be anything that will touch God's heart more than to be firm in the belief, as I am, that the crucified Christ was made man in order to show what men should be like? *suddenly jumping up in fear* What will happen to the children in future, to Christl, little blind Christl? Has anyone among you seen her? I left the child behind in a place where, as in a paradise, sorrow, hunger and misery had spared the land. I left her with our patron, young Prince Rakoczy, hoping that divine providence would change its mind about the catastrophe of the religious wars, about the end of mankind.

DRABIK *appearing from the background, ghostly, like a seer* The Prince and Princess died of the plague. In the castle crypt I laid them on their bier and draped the catafalque in black cloth. As is the custom, old women kissed the dead monarchs on the forehead. I also let the children approach, they wanted to see how the dry air in the crypt had conserved the corpses, as if they would get up at any moment. Was it not you yourself who taught the children that all wisdom comes from seeing and understanding?

COMENIUS *falling to his knees* Merciful Lord! The plague! Where is Christl?

DRABIK Let me continue. The Prince and Princess were children too, human beings even though they were nobles, and if death had not reformed them, they would have run away from you when they reached maturity, just like others. Twice I had to tie up the Prince's jaw with a cloth so that the blowflies would not spread the plague.

COMENIUS Our patron dead! God have mercy on him. But where is Christl? It is three years to the day now since I left the blind child in the care of you — you who can see into the future! — in a place where, in view of the misery in the rest of the world, a benevolent providence could take precautions. Another blow! The plague in

Hungary! But where is the child? Her mother was Jewish. In order to save the child from pogroms, I called her Christl.

DRABIK *takes a long, slow drink drink from a bottle of schnapps, after offering it to Comenius, who refuses it* Not on the catafalque with the dolled-up couple who are now putrefying. The smell of someone decaying is worse than that of the common man. I left your Christl with the blind, the lame, and the cripples who put their infirmities on show outside the castle and the church, on order to arouse people's pity. Have a drink, Pastor, schnapps keeps your innards warmer than a sermon on liberty, equality and fraternity. *handing the bottle round, encouraging the crowd to drink*

THE CROWD Truly, that Drabik's a fine fellow, even the Devil respects him.

DRABIK *to Comenius* Why did Christ not stay in the pulpit, a learned preacher, instead of taking a stick and driving the merchants and moneychangers out of the temple.

COMENIUS *cries out, sobbing* What has happened to the blind child?

DRABIK Patience, Pastor, the children of our time have become as cautious as foxes and as cunning as snakes. No coffin-maker will be able to tell you under which stone Christl is resting, with her name, fine words and in everlasting peace, court jester to the prince whose ribs will even now be sticking out of his ceremonial robes. She refused to be separated from the corpse of the papist dragoon who, so I heard, was protecting her. She didn't need my hand, she said, nor that of the old teacher, nor did she believe in the Son of God, in whose name the war was being fought. She was going to clean the stones under which her lover lay, even if the wind should cover them with dust a thousand times over. She lodges in the brick shed that she goes back to every night like a bat.

ACT THREE

SCENE ONE

The ante-room to the audience chamber of the royal palace in Stockholm

COMENIUS *some of the Brethren are waiting nervously; de Geert rushes in, pale and distraught* You bring us bad news from the Castle, Brother?

DE GEERT Unfortunately confirmation has been received of the rumor that the Duke of Friedland, Wallenstein, has been murdered, in Eger. The Inquisition denounced him at the court in Vienna; they claimed he was seeking the crown of Bohemia for himself.

COMENIUS God be with us! Yet still I refuse to despair, now that the Reformation has torn down the walls separating the most distant peoples, Sweden here, Bohemia there. The peoples are becoming citizens of the world. The solidarity which one often denies one's own neighbors in times of need is becoming a rallying cry for the Brethren, now, when people are even fighting against their own countrymen for freedom.

DE GEERT Bohemia has been lost since Gustavus Adolphus, the most feared enemy of Habsburg and Spain, fell in battle last year. His daughter, the Queen, wants to make peace with Habsburg because Cardinal Richelieu is refusing Sweden any more subsidies.

COMENIUS But the Cardinal sent word to me only recently that he approved of my idea of setting up a pansophic college in Paris. The justice of our cause means that even reasons of state unite the liberal nations. The dove of peace from Noah's Ark flew out over the Flood. In ancient times the Egyptian princess saved the infant Moses, floating in his rush basket on the mud of the river of death. And the dove of peace led me to Fulnek where soldiers, the cross in one hand, a musket in the other, stormed the houses, without first of all going in by the door, as even a dog would do. A child, Christl, lay crying for mercy in the bleeding arms of her mother, whose body had been cut to pieces. It is not because of the religious conflict, it is because of the children that I am seeking an audience here with Queen Christina.

Lackeys open the double doors to the audience chamber.

QUEEN CHRISTINA *seated, Oxenstierna standing, holding a document in his hands, undecided. Comenius is admitted. The Queen turns toward him, impatiently signing the document Oxenstierna places on the table* We are of the opinion that undivided peace, a great idea, certainly, will remain an illusion. It will take time before the human comedy in this labyrinth of the world of error can be recognized for the tragedy it is.

OXENSTIERNA *to Comenius* My sovereign is minded to make a start with educating our own people to use their reason, employing your method, Bishop Comenius. However, we do not intend to waste the money we won in the war on a utopian dream. Our country has become short of men, they are scattered all over the world, the land is untilled. Our Treasury therefore, in order to demonstrate our Queen's sympathy for your plan, has orders to put five hundred thalers per year at your disposal, as long as you remain in our country to teach.

COMENIUS From the bottom of my heart I thank your Highness. The children with their pretty verses will be better able to express their gratitude to your Majesty's government for appointing teachers from afar off to turn inexperienced children into adult human beings, ripe for peace. But there is a rumor going round that Bohemia is to be betrayed in the Peace of Westphalia?

QUEEN *in vehement response* Even the French Cardinal is ready now to put an end to the religious discord. Even France is exhausted.

In Thorn the assembled shepherds of the Christian flocks, as well as those who steer the ships of state, will agree on a formula which will put an end to the theological conflict, and encourage the disaffected peasants to return to their beasts and their fields. This we, as Queen of Sweden, are firmly resolved upon.

COMENIUS *on his knees before her* By all Christ's wounds, I beseech you, our royal patroness, not to abandon my people, who are being persecuted for their faith.

OXENSTIERNA *speaking in support of Comenius* A peace that satisfies neither the Protestants nor the Papists can only lead to new wars. It would be a dishonorable peace which will merely compel Sweden to withdraw from Germany in order to make room for the French King. The Pope in Rome himself is against this peace.

QUEEN After all the years of bloodshed, the religious conflict has turned Europe into a slaughterhouse. It proves how pointless it is to try to settle differences of opinion by the sword; the end result is that St. Peter will return home empty-handed from his fishing trip and Richelieu will fleece the patient German lamb instead of Oxenstierna. After the death of our glorious father we, Christina of Sweden, are minded to put your plan, Bishop Comenius, before the rulers of the states. With time, human reason will become ripe for peace.

DE GEERT *hesitantly speaking from the line of supplicants to Comenius* . . . and I advise you, father, not to stay in Sweden, but to go to Thorn and face the theological foxes, so that the Unity of Brethren will not be alone in speaking for the freedom of Bohemia.

COMENIUS I am exhausted, the years of my old age are approaching. However, your gracious Majesty, it is not old age but fear for my brethren that makes my legs shake, and that is why I must go to Thorn, to the conference of bishops.

QUEEN *severely* We will see to it that, in return for the payment of subsidies, the Unity of the Bohemian Brethren, who are now scattered all over the world, will release you from your duties. We repeat: your plan to educate the nations to use their reason we will put before the representatives of the governments and the churches gathered in Thorn, with our special recommendation that they look on it favorably. Now go in God's name and take up your office as a teacher in Sweden.

COMENIUS *leaves sadly* I look to Him who feeds the birds under the heavens for my reward.

DE GEERT *leaving with him, with a cry of despair* And I say you must go to Thorn. Remember Bishop Chelcicky's fury when he said how the colonel who teaches the art of killing is richly rewarded while the schoolmaster, who does humanity a much greater service, is barely allowed enough to keep body and soul together.

OXENSTIERNA *takes from the table the document the Queen has signed, reads it, and falls to his knees before her* My Queen! Your signature on the treaty of the Peace of Westphalia! In the name of the sorrows Our Lord suffered on the cross, reconsider your decision! In the name of all those who have died in this war for the Protestant faith, on my knees I beg for mercy from your Majesty, whose education it was for so long my privilege to direct.

QUEEN *at first moved, then in a firm voice* Bishop Comenius' closest associate has just now agreed to support the work of peace in Thorn. Oxenstierna, we regard you as our friend, and thank you for all the good you did for us when we spent our childhood alone, as if in a cage, or with dwarves and fools, while my mother, involved in intrigues regarding the succession, tried to betroth me to any number of candidates for the throne, all of whom were equally hateful to me.

OXENSTIERNA *looking round cautiously* The Spanish envoy is at the door, asking for audience. I would rather hear the last trump than be witness to your Majesty's volte-face. If you now surrender Bohemia, which with French help it is still in our power to liberate, to the mercy of the Habsburgs, for what, then, did your great father give his life? For a cause which you are now throwing away, as if it was all a game! It was in the name of the Allies, but, above all, with his dear blood, that he promised that nation its freedom. And now this black-haired Spaniard wants to persuade you that Bohemia should not be granted Christ's peace, as we understand it. Could it be feminine sensibility has seduced your Majesty into this aberration?

QUEEN *growing angry* Chancellor! Since our childhood you have commanded our deepest respect, but our ears are tired of your constant urgings in favor of Bohemia, which is forever keeping the world in a state of unrest and conflict. Since you mention our sex, then know that, although you are our Chancellor, our personal relations with the Spanish envoy are none of your business. I may make him my lover, but never my spouse, no more than the Protestant princes they keep presenting to me, least of all your son, Count Oxenstierna! And that despite the fact that, for political reasons, even the King of France supports that marriage.

OXENSTIERNA *Trying to rise* My Queen, permit your servant, who seems too old for his task, to give you back his seals of office.

QUEEN *helps Oxenstierna to his feet, kisses his forehead, sobbing* Arise, Chancellor. No longer Count, but Prince Oxenstierna. That is our will. And your son shall take over the reins of government from you, while we go to Rome to follow the progress of the extension of St. Peter's. We will not allow our friend to leave us in an ill humor. You can be reassured, Prince Oxenstierna; the only truth behind the fact that we are leaving for Rome in the company of the Spanish envoy, is that we are all made of flesh and blood, even a queen. Now keep your moralizing, my dearest subject and my friend. The only truth about the intrigues with the Holy See is that even in Rome young people kiss each other without a priest's blessing. Just now it must be so delectably balmy beneath the fig trees in Tivoli that one wants to hold one's breath to make the night last longer, to listen to the nightingales before dawn breaks.

OXENSTIERNA *wrestling with his conscience, signs the peace treaty and leaves the audience chamber through a side door.*

QUEEN *rings a bell*

THE SPANISH ENVOY *enters, bowing to the ground, accompanied by lackeys who set up a marble statue of a naked female, at the moment still veiled, before the Queen.* Will your gracious and youthful Majesty deign to accept a present from the Holy Father, that was only recently dug up in the eternal city? It is our sacred Mother Earth alone which gives birth to such miracles, while in their fatherlands men and women twist and turn in their sleep, as if dreaming feverish dreams. This goddess from antiquity is a messenger from the Holy Father welcoming the Virgin Queen. *unveils the statue*

QUEEN *gazing dreamily at the statue in admiration* Prince, you are an interesting European, coming to us as you do with a work of art instead of with weapons. Our country is poor in works of art, and to our great sorrow, one of our warships, laden with art treasures from Germany, recently sank in Stockholm harbor.

THE SPANISH ENVOY To my great regret, on my long journey from Rome, where I was born, I encountered nothing but ruins, more destruction and ugliness than one would have thought mankind capable of causing. If the armies of those fighting for the Protestant faith could have put out the sun, they would have done so. According to the theologians, the secular scholars too have now shifted our mother earth from the center of creation to the rank of an ordinary star. A complete denial of Providence's creation, is that the way to prepare for the empire of eternal peace? However, in Rome a new movement is starting, a counterreformation, in which people are bold enough to break open the walls of the inner chamber of the temple, raising them into a dome as high as the clouds, from where light will begin to pour into the abode of the dark god. People do not want to see a dead man hanging on the cross any more, they want their patron goddess with the olive branch to come with her gentle power. Your Majesty, come to Rome! Where the people build pleasure domes in the churches in the name of the merciful Mother of God.

QUEEN *with a laugh* Pleasure domes! Castles in Spain more like! If it were the will of Providence to use a queen to bring tormented humanity back together in one family, we would gladly lay our crown at the feet of the Mother of God. Our heart is not set on power. Our crown did not come to us by the grace of God, but from our late father. Prince, you must know that we do not believe in miracles, but that life is given us to be lived. For that reason we do not believe in consecrated wafers either, which are not sufficient to feed the hungry. We will not make a pact with the Holy Father, although you are his best mediator. Perhaps the doctors at the universities can shift the heavens, but even the Pope cannot open the gates of heaven with money. And the people cannot put their human nature behind them; if they go hungry, they are filled with wrath. That is why they go to war.

THE SPANISH ENVOY My love! Come to Rome with me! Where the old stones protect the populace — the most unruly, the most rebellious of all people — against attacks by the Huns, Goths, Saracens, against earthquake and flood. The church militant has made a refuge for the Queen of Heaven, who offers her breast to the child playing with the lamb in the Garden of Eden. Catholic artists from all over the world are creating a picture of the Visitation of Our Lady in the temple. To celebrate the end of the war, the Holy Father has introduced the Feast of the Holy Rosary in honor of the Virgin Mary.

QUEEN I repeat, the people cannot put their human nature behind them, if they feel oppressed, they rebel. Look: my foot hurts, and immediately I start to get angry with my shoe. Certainly it would be lovely to dream of a kingdom here in the icy north, shut away like Sleeping Beauty's castle from the horrors of war, to bind a busy swarm of artists to us, in order to mend the breaches the guns of the Pope and our late father made in the world.

THE SPANISH ENVOY All that needs to be done is to abjure this abstract faith that abhors images and whose justification only comes with death.

QUEEN Do you believe, Prince, that salvation is impossible for a person who rends the veil of abstract reason, on the wall behind which there are only pictures — intangible pictures — of the imagination?

THE SPANISH ENVOY Madame, if only I were permitted to kiss your foot! You have poured so much charm on an unworthy man.

QUEEN *deeply moved, embraces him* We shall go to Rome. You are so delightfully insistent, but your Virgin on the sickle moon almost makes us jealous. We ought to go to a convent so that she can open the gates of paradise for us. And we would love to see the works the artists have created in honor of the holy Virgin. But the work one would rather call the greatest would be one painted for the love of a mortal woman. My unforgettable friend, do the beautiful women of Rome not complain that they are ignored? What a burden to wear a crown! Almost unbearable for a woman whose heart is full of tender feelings. These endless nights when the owl's plaintive cry will not let us sleep, these bright nights full of longing! How strange that men all chase after unattainable ideals. Prince, do you demand more from us than we are able to give?

THE SPANISH ENVOY The Queen crying! *falls at her feet*

QUEEN *raising him up* Curb your passion! The etiquette of our court does not allow such behavior. The woman in me forgives you, but the queen will revile you till her dying day for promising her a paradise of the heart. Go now. I shall never forget you. Outside, the sun is thawing the icy landscape. Government business calls the Queen.

ACT FOUR

Amsterdam, spring afternoon in Rembrandt's studio; the painter is poor, but cheerful; there are many pictures stacked up in piles and portfolios with engravings leaning against the wall; an old bed in one corner; dust and squalor. The "Night Watch" is on the easel, darkly glowing in a shaft of storm-shot light. Rembrandt has been working on it, he is stomping angrily round the floor, where he has thrown down his brushes and palette. He tears the head-scarf off his half-bald pate and flails away wildly at the flies. He clutches at his heart, then grabs the empty schnapps bottle and throws it out of the window.

REMBRANDT *at the window* Hendrijke!

HENDRIJKE *outside* What d'you want, Rembrandt?

REMBRANDT Schnapps!

HENDRIJKE No swilling schnapps in the middle of the day! There's someone knocking at the door.

REMBRANDT *slams the window shut* Damned flies! I can already see pink elephants in the picture. As if my own eyes were betraying me! Still broad daylight. Little children, flowers in their hair, are playing ring-around-a-rosy with the seven little kids, and hide-and-seek in the moonlight round the boots of those swashbuckling bravos there! *glares at the picture* Didn't Hendrijke have some money left? Where can she have hidden it? My brain put up a stout fight against collapse, but spasms of fear have been stabbing at my heart ever since.

He adds a few more strokes to the picture, then goes to the bed in the corner and rummages about underneath it. The door opens and Hendrijke comes in, catching Rembrandt in the act.

HENDRIJKE Rembrandt! What are you looking for there? There's someone asking for you.

REMBRANDT *embarrassed* Hendrijke, please, don't think I'm trying to pretend I'm better than I am.

HENDRIJKE *forcefully* I'm going to leave you! If Saskia were still alive I wouldn't go with you!

REMBRANDT *grinning, laughing* I've seen better days, too. Only a common miller's son, yet I could play the nobleman, and my poor Saskia took my braggart's word at face value. I ran up debts for the most delicate creature in the world; I dressed her in silks and satins, I hung gold and pearls round her neck. Just between you and me, before the war the Netherlands were rolling in money. Everyone was happy to make loans to the bridegroom of the daughter of a wealthy patrician like Saskia.

HENDRIJKE *out of breath* I'm going back home tomorrow! *bursting into tears* O Rembrandt, if only you weren't so helpless! *picks up the paints and brushes from the floor and fastens his turban for him* It's irritating rather than hurtful. *takes the money he had put in his pocket* If it had been a little baby that the prattling players at the fair pull out from under their jackets at the right moment to soften up their audience, it wouldn't have made his jacket as dirty as this money getting somewhere it didn't belong! *makes the bed again* And a beautiful woman like Saskia had to die for a slovenly pig like that. *Comenius appears in the doorway.*

REMBRANDT *in friendly tones* Don't be crazy. Let's talk like rational people, instead of this blubbering. Since you've been running the business in your own name the usurers have left me in peace, I admit. Of course it wouldn't be the same for me any more, I'm very sloppy at running a household. It's not food that keeps us alive. I find it difficult to bring myself to say it, but I admit that taking the money was a nasty trick to play. And as far as my liking

you is concerned . . . can a simple woman understand that? *becoming more and more ridiculous, speaking like a complete fool who is adopting a pose and declaiming* You are not the kind of person who would go to another man just because he was younger and better. Yes, in matters of the heart you are as genuine as a diamond from Jewry Lane, and you are the only person left in the world who regards Rembrandt van Rijn in his rags and tatters as a grand gentleman. *laughing and crying* Rembrandt, a gentleman who steals!
Comenius has entered the room unnoticed

HENDRIJKE *won over, but even more irritated* All your silly twaddle just makes me angry, it makes me furious, if you want to know the truth. *pointing to Comenius* I thought it was the doctor, come for his money, whether he managed to do anything for the dropsy you've had since last fall or not. To hell with your money, my money, it's ours! There are lots of people who secretly appropriate things that don't belong to them and wouldn't dream of calling it theft, but that's the respectable people in the town. You don't need to make a fool of yourself in front of the stranger here. Now, do up your trousers and welcome our visitor.
Comenius stays in the background, leafing through the portfolios of prints

REMBRANDT *whistling in order to hide his emotion; he tries to catch a large bluebottle that has been irritating him all the time* Well, Hendrijke, you could wait a little longer and see how things turn out, don't you think? *finally catches the fly; stammering* That's all quite natural, but, you see, we're here now, aren't we, and then we're gone in a flash? *lightheartedly and in a cheerful mood again* Dead, even poor old Rembrandt won't be a sight to be ashamed of any more, however much he drank while he was still alive. When I'm gone, write on my grave, schnapps and sorrow swallowed up Rembrandt as the ocean did the sailor. Of course, if you really mean to go, I'm happy to make it easier for you. *lets the fly go out of the window, which he then shuts* Off you go, poor thing, see that you find some better place. There's room for everything in the world

HENDRIJKE *getting more agitated again* It's not a sin any more that I gave something of my own, something I can dispose of myself, my body, whenever you were close to despair in your black moods. No, it's myself I find killingly funny. Our penury and squalor seems of so little importance to you, as if it didn't concern you or me. Even flies mean more to you. That this stranger might mock me as the burghers of Amsterdam did, that doesn't bother me; didn't they ridicule the great Rembrandt in the days when he thought he was still one of them. But that Rembrandt, starving and ill and dying, that you should secretly steal the few thalers I have managed to scrape together, steal them from me, a poor countrywoman who would give you her own breast to suck at to keep you alive, just in order to poison yourself with schnapps — who can see that happening and still believe in God? *in fury, she throws the coins onto the floor* Since Sodom and Gomorrah there hasn't been a woman so petrified as I was, watching him amuse himself confessing his basest actions, as if the only thing that concerned him was to show himself up before this stranger! Rembrandt van Rijn! I don't understand myself any more, but one thing I do know: if you are ridiculed for it, that will be the deepest humiliation my heart has had to suffer. *picks up the money from the floor, is about to go away, then remembers their visitor*

COMENIUS Do you think he'll listen to me now? Rembrandt van Rijn! My Brethren think you should paint a portrait of me. If you would just look at me . . . life is ebbing away beneath the snow of my hair . . .

HENDRIJKE *now fully the businesswoman serving a customer, obsequiously wiping the only chair clean* Rembrandt, take the gentleman's hat and stick. *to Comenius* The painter will be delighted to fix your honor's likeness on canvas. If he seems distracted, it is just that he is committing your honor's features to memory. In the meantime I will set up the background. That's the Watch that the burghers of Amsterdam refuse to take because the dimensions are wrong for City Hall. *in a low voice to Rembrandt* Rembrandt! You heard! The man wants his picture done. Remember there's no cabbage left in the larder.

REMBRANDT *so far completely unaffected by Comenius' presence* The difficulty is that, if one needs money, the only answer to that is "yes," and not "no." Do not take it amiss, Mynheer, that you witnessed a domestic conversation, that, too, might have been predestined. *looks bewildered, like a child that has just been woken up, then he cannot repress a laugh*

COMENIUS Yes. To return to the commission of my Brethren, is there something funny about it I can't see?

REMBRANDT *ushers Comenius to the chair, picks up a sketching pencil* Typical Hendrijke. Nothing matters as long as we don't run out of greens. I could be an atheist, for all she cares. You can see from her face that she's the incarnation of unselfishness, while we, if there were nowhere else free, would happily paint our pictures on the Creator's own nose, just like the flies. And she just carries on, wearing herself to the bone. She wouldn't hold it against me if I stripped the clothes from her body and sold them for schnapps. *shouting* Hendrijke! Some light! It's getting dark!

COMENIUS *referring to Hendrijke, who has just left*
The Kingdom of Heaven will be ours, if we can take off our mask and not feel ashamed.

REMBRANDT *as the darkness increases; confiding tone* Since you quote the Scriptures — although I am no friend of those sanctimonious humbugs who call on God and the Bible as witness every time they open their mouths, yet I like your honest eyes. What was I going to say? Oh, yes. I know our fathers' Scriptures as well as any child its own home; even better: as if everything had happened to me myself. The way the most fantastical as well as the most heartwarming stories are told with all the graphic power of the word makes it clear to us that art should not be used to prettify or disguise things. But Holy Writ will still allow an honest fellow, whose head swims at the nothingness of the world, an occasional pause for breath. And it's dark, the world today, I tell you. Hope is like a ray of light that only rarely flits across the darkness; the Jews understood that and turned it into unforgettable human history. Their neighbors, the Greeks, carved it in stone with their chisels. What respect those ancients must have had for their descendants to entrust them with that inheritance! Hey, you're closing your eyes, my friend!

COMENIUS *had dropped off to sleep; smiles as if in a dream, rubs his eyes in embarrassment* Ah, the painter's spirit, more fortunate than ordinary mortals, you shovel up pearls and gold from the dust of your studio, on your wings you carry us up in a dream along the Via Lucis . . . *stands up; it has grown dark. Outside in the street the sound of troops marching, a drum.* If only the world were merely a vision of light and shade, merely our imagination! Anyone who's spent his life coming up against one brick wall after another knows that's not the case.

REMBRANDT *stops working* Hendrijke! Trim the candle! *to Comenius* Devil take the Town Guard, marching along with all their noise! I still owe the money for the canvas and paints for their picture. I compounded for the money, you could even say I sold myself, if you like to put it that way. *moving the picture more to the front of the stage* My house in the town came under the hammer, everything carried off. My creditors had the upper hand. Then this commission from the arquebusiers seemed to be our salvation. But it looks as if, since then, nothing but mold has been growing in my paintpots. *turning to Comenius, in more friendly tones* There's something about you that encourages one to speak . . . *putting his hand over his mouth and indicating the Watch* . . . one's mind freely. *adopting a comic pose, making fun of the good burghers in their knights' costumes, brandishing his brush like a sword* Try

Comenius 235

telling these fire-eaters here that on them their knights' armor looks as if they had stolen it from the nobles. Your captain there, aren't those painted lips of his saying, "Look at me, Jan Turkeycock, Captain of the Cloveniersdoelen, the Guild of Arquebusiers, with the claw of the Liberty Cock in his cap! Aren't I just the hero!" If someone had the audacity to call our civil liberties a farthing dip to his face, the grumbler would be lucky to get away without having a firebrand tossed onto his roof.
Hendrikje sets a tallow candle on the table. Rembrandt spits on the floor at the feet of the Watch, goes to the table, which is not yet set, and chomps away noisily at a raw onion.
Today the hearts of our burghers are set out on the market stalls for sale to the highest bidder, but their lips are dribbling with patriotism. *Comenius takes a closer look at the picture, which is getting very dark; Rembrandt goes to the window* I'll open the window just a crack for you. We expect to hear the rowdies making their racket outside. The Jews are celebrating their Easter festival just as we do. They fled from Spain, but their fleeces they had to leave behind them. *trying to entertain Comenius* The Town Guard, whose portrait I've painted here, look more like the lost souls to whom the Savior descended. It needs a ray of light. I just can't finish the picture off. I need an inspiration! *turning away from the picture* It's not for nothing that the people mock me by calling me the painter of light and shade. You're a schoolteacher. I've read your reforms for children's education. Full of optimism, you pick out reason as the light that leads out of the labyrinth of the world and into the paradise of the future. Children's education, yes! But although you can't get more into an adult's head than it will take, every skull always has enough room to build castles in the air. Even the divine Plato, who played a trick on the ancient philosophers by declaring ideas the model of all creation, could not create a world different from the one that exists. Nevertheless, I wish you luck for your planned school, just as in a story, which can only have a happy or an unhappy end, once it's told. Sit down, my friend. What good fortune, that you, who plan to teach mankind to see and to understand, should come to me, who am looking for inspiration. A spiritual light! *pointing to an*

empty place in the picture of the Watch Here! What people call classical antiquity taught the so-called facts of nature, but not what mankind is. Now the Bible . . . *outside, the sound of a drum-roll quite close to the house* Like flies, they are. But the Jews on the other hand, you have to grant that, unlike us Christians, and despite persecution, the Ghetto, and the yellow patch they have to wear, they have not lost their human dignity. No lip-service to a God whom they only start to believe in when he has become a son of man like the rest of us. That's why they can make war in God's name with impunity. Just as the Anabaptists buy themselves their rebirth with immersion in water, so do the Christians their resurrection in the world hereafter. Bad conscience, that's the trouble with us, that's why we don't feel at home in the world. In the hereafter, in a better future, tomorrow, but not today!

HENDRIJKE *coming out of the kitchen, flushed* Our visitor didn't ask, but I've cooked for three hungry people all the same. The gentleman must have seen better days too. There's no need to feel ashamed, you always find poor people at Rembrandt's table. Poor folk are just like flies, they like to eat together. Whether you're a Jew or a Christian *with a laugh* you won't break any rules of fasting with our fare. *becoming more friendly with their silent guest* Perhaps the gentleman is a rabbi? A lot of them come to us from the Empire nowadays. *serving up the food* In these modern days God is farther away than ever. He can't concern himself with everyone if even their neighbors won't. *with a laugh* But sit yourself down, you must be tired. You must think I'm nothing but a simpleton. *all three sit down at the table*

COMENIUS *in a weary voice* For over forty years now I've been wandering from land to land, like Ahasuerus, preaching to deaf ears, unrecognized, and homesick for the country where I was born and where I have been forgotten: Bohemia, ravaged and despoiled by foreign mercenaries. People take my teachings for a mirage that deludes people who are dying of thirst in the desert. My name is Jan

Amos Comenius. I am a schoolmaster. *pats Rembrandt's wife on the shoulder*

REMBRANDT *urging him to eat* Help yourself to what we have to offer a guest. Cabbage. The farmer who sowed and harvested it, dealt with it in the same way as he deals with his enemies: they also only have one head each on their shoulders. Remember Caesar, who was a demigod. He had the right hand of tens of thousands of my forefathers chopped off. Then along came Brutus. Eat your cabbage up before it gets cold. We eat to stay alive.

COMENIUS *breaking his silence and getting worked up* I'm not hungry. I feel like a cook who prepares tasty dishes for others, but doesn't eat his fill himself. This world is devoid of reason, and I feel like turning my back on it, however deeply I felt for humanity during the thirty years of warfare I was working out my plan for schools. I have presented it to parliaments and statesmen in many countries, but in vain. I have to admit that in the modern age people have started learning to read and write a little again, and to use calculus, but for all that the world seems to be sinking even deeper and deeper into barbarism. The dawn of the human spirit was indeed a mirage that left the thirsty people to die in the desert. The greed, in which people are like wild animals, and their thoughtlessness, in which they resemble a herd of sheep following the bellwether over a cliff, have become worse in our reformed age. War will never end! The states barter their people as if they were beasts in a slaughterhouse. Squalor and crime will never end. On the contrary, in their haste everyone is trying to grab what they can of natural resources, without thinking of future generations. The world is a hell. We keep putting off our destiny of a fully developed humanity to a later date, just as the Church puts off eternal peace to a hereafter, to a future that will never arrive. The clock is standing still. They all say the time is not ripe. I believe that mankind will die out, just as the giants and dinosaurs of prehistoric times did, unless we come to reason. *pushes his plate away from him, brooding*

REMBRANDT *trying to cheer him up* My dear friend, look, instead of turning your back on the world, why don't you return to your classroom where the board is meant to be black! Have patience. Look at nature: a chick stands on its feet and pecks for its food the moment it comes out of the egg. Accept the world the way it is! A human child needs nine months before it comes into the world, and years to learn to walk and to speak. And with all that my poor Titus did not live to see what fate might have had in store for him. As far as time is concerned, the fact is that it is merely an illusion. On mature consideration, perhaps the world itself is nothing but appearances, light or dark, depending on the way you see it.

HENDRIJKE If you're going to chatter on and on, let me get the table cleared. I would get depressed if I felt I had to spend all my time thinking profound thoughts. In the end a huge broom sweeps through the house, and that's another one finished. *she puts a bottle of schnapps on the table; Rembrandt pours a glass for himself and one for Comenius, who waves it away* I was keeping the schnapps hidden for that good-for-nothing tonight. Look how he's brightened up already. You can pore over as many dusty old tomes as you like, you still can't put it better than my Savior at the Lord's Supper, "This is my body, my blood, for ever and ever, amen."

COMENIUS *waking from his musing* For ever and ever, my good woman? You have eternity right in front of your nose, the sea you can see there across the turf takes the just and the unjust, without letting either trouble it, just as the ocean does the sailor. *standing up, preparing to leave* There's no advantage to you in having fed me, a refugee living on the world's pity. Even eternity is not interested in thanks from a man whose reason tells him what an ephemeral being he is, too ephemeral to believe he was created in God's image. Whether Papist or Protestant, man should apologize if he believes in an omnipotent creator who can hear him.

HENDRIJKE *looking toward the window because she has heard someone knocking at it* Another of those children wandering around late at night? *opening the window a little*

CHILD'S VOICE Could I just pop in for a moment to see Rembrandt?

REMBRANDT *jumping up, opening the door a little* That's Hannah, Shylock's foster daughter. *to the child* Quick!! Come in! A little Jewish girl like you can slip more easily through the eye of a needle than a Protestant Mynheer through the gates of heaven. Have you come to Rembrandt to pour your heart out to him?

HANNAH *a little girl in a white dress, with a wreath of flowers and a veil on her head; at first she edges in timidly round the door then runs over to the easel, where it is dark* Rembrandt! Shylock sends you a silk handkerchief for your birthday. *a child's arm is visible, holding out the handkerchief to Rembrandt*

REMBRANDT *arms outstretched, vainly trying to catch her in the dark. Comenius, excited, also goes toward the picture, where he thinks the girl is hiding* Come out of the darkness, otherwise one of those fire-eaters might tread on your toes. The tears are running down my cheeks. Shylock the Jew was the only one to remember my birthday. *showing the handkerchief to Comenius* Such a fine handkerchief for my honest, snotty, Low-German nose, which people insult by calling it degenerate.

COMENIUS *waves Rembrandt away, runs round the easel, reappears in the foreground* I'm looking for the girl. You called her Hannah.

REMBRANDT *clapping his hands and calling out loud*
Hannah! Shylock's praying in the synagogue, you can't stay at home by yourself. I'll keep you here with us for the night, you'll be as safe as a dove in a dovecote. *calling out to Hendrijke in the kitchen*

Hendrijke! Two times two is four, they taught us at school. We need another cabbage, there's four of us.

CHILD'S VOICE Rembrandt! Don't think I'm being rude, but I can't stay. Tonight the Jews will turn the tablets of the law over, so as not to annoy the Christians, who are also celebrating Easter. Of all the girls, the rabbi chose me to recite a poem in the synagogue. The synagogue is full of the scent of cedars of Lebanon. I'm really looking forward to it, but I'm awfully frightened, too, whether I'll remember the poem. If only it were over! *reappearing in front of the canvas; takes Rembrandt by the arm and whispers to him secretly* I'll recite it to you alone first, after the gentleman's gone. It's a secret, only for your ears! I can't stay long. *turns back to the canvas*

COMENIUS *goes to leave, but stops by the door, as if he were waiting for the child* But that's the child I'm looking for! The one I took from the arms of her dying mother. Christl I christened her. *out loud* Child . . . I would have left of my own accord, but no person is in another's way if he still has something to learn. I used to teach children, in my old age I could learn something from a child. I'm a friend of the painter. Who are you, child? You can trust me, even though I don't wear the Jew's patch. My foreign dress is cause enough for people to throw stones at me. You're a clever girl, Hannah? or Christl? Do you understand? Nowadays they play with people just as a child satisfies its curiosity playing with a toy until it breaks.

HANNAH *only indistinctly visible* How foolish people can be! Though, of course, I've never been outside the Ghetto. Shylock has promised to send me to the town school when I'm older, so that I will get to know some Christians. *appearing in the foreground for the last time; close to Rembrandt* Don't let me keep you, sir. We will see each other on the way. I've got wings on the soles of my feet, just like a fairy tale, I'll easily catch up with you.

COMENIUS *going out of the door* Don't hold me back, Rembrandt. I've lived long enough to know that I can trust children.

REMBRANDT *peering anxiously out of the window into the street, where it seems to be quite quiet now* Just remember! Your children's school is hardly a generation old. Be careful in the streets. *aside* The Jews have been learning how to stay alive for two thousand years. I can rely on Hannah. The really clever people say this is a time of transition. *laughs out loud*

VOICE *of one of the Watch heard through the open door; they have stopped Comenius* Halt! What are you doing in the street at this late hour, when honest citizens are asleep in their beds? *the soldiers bring Comenius back to the door*

COMENIUS I can't sleep while dreams of peace are raging inside me, have done all my life. I'm searching for a child, still.

REMBRANDT *approaches the group, about to intervene*

COMENIUS *to Rembrandt* Do not hold me back, my friend, I am old enough to deal with people.

ONE OF THE WATCH *reporting to the captain* Captain, the man seized by the officers of the law is abroad in the Jewish quarter without having the prescribed yellow patch on his coat.

CAPTAIN *to Comenius* Are you one of the tolerated Jews of Amsterdam? Your papers! How much money do you have on you?

COMENIUS *in friendly tones* No money and no papers, I have to admit.

CAPTAIN *to the soldiers* Take the old man away. To the police station. Seems to be a suspicious character. Speak up, I can't understand you.

242 *Comenius*

REMBRANDT *can control himself no longer; tries to pull Comenius away from the guards* Leave the old man alone, *his voice has grown hoarse, like that of everyone who has been crying out for freedom.* He is a refugee and my guest. What will they say about our hospitality abroad?

CAPTAIN I thought so. A refugee taking the bread out of the mouths of our citizens in this time of crisis. The war's on again! And you, Rembrandt, don't stick your nose into things that don't concern you, don't try to obstruct the law. You'll be hearing from us.

The Watch leaves with Comenius, Rembrandt slams the door angrily; it grows quite dark in the studio. Rembrandt is busying himself in front of the easel, he can be heard grumbling, but is not visible. Thunderstorm, lightning.

REMBRANDT My honest, Low-German nose was good enough for the Jew Shylock to remember my birthday.
Stage fills with smoke.

CHILD'S VOICE Rembrandt! Can you hear me?

REMBRANDT I can't find my way in this smoke. It can't come from the bottle, the bottle's empty. *he can be heard flinging it onto the floor*

CHILD'S VOICE *second time, at a higher pitch* Rembrandt! Can you hear me?

REMBRANDT *shouting to the kitchen* Hendrijke! Schnapps!

CHILD'S VOICE *third time* Rembrandt! Can you hear me? Like the princess, locked away in her castle until this day, Jehovah's pure maid puts her request to Him whose spirit, softly, miraculously becomes the breath of all creatures. *her voice rises, rejoicing, to the*

highest pitch Princess, for the rite of spring there awakes a human being whose slavery is at an end!
The empty space in the painting of the Watch begins to glow, the whole picture becoming clearer.

REMBRANDT *losing his composure, beside himself, feeling for a chair* Hannah, where are you? Who are you?
Daybreak. The mysterious girl, who is unrelated to the burghers in their fancy dress, can be clearly seen painted on the picture of the Night Watch.

CHILD'S VOICE Your guest's wanderings are over. He died in the street. Hannah, whom he called Christl in order to save a child from mankind, is accompanying him into the hereafter. In your picture I am there as witness to his compassion, showing to all what being human means.

HENDRIJKE *rushing into the studio and putting out the tallow candle* Just look at that! I could have saved the copper for the candle, not to mention the cabbage in the cellar. You painted the picture in the dark. For me it's a miracle, and I'm not ashamed to say so!

AFTERWORD

Oskar Kokoschka (1886-1980) is a leading representative of an extraordinarily talented generation of German-speaking artists, writers and intellectuals. They were born into a stable world of the late nineteenth century but saw their view of the self transformed by the new psychology of Sigmund Freud and their world torn apart by ideological, political and military conflict in the early twentieth century. Rebelling against the values of the *Bildungsbürgertum* or educated middle classes, which had been forced upon them in the rigid school system, Kokoschka's generation rejected the conservative social and aesthetic norms of their parents. The result of that rebellion was the movement in art and literature known as Expressionism. Its beginnings are usually dated around 1907-1910. It peaked in the middle of the second decade and fizzled out in the early 1920s, not least because so many of its principal representatives had lost their lives in the First World War. In literature, the Expressionists rejected what they regarded as the stifling Realism of conventional literature. Instead, they sought to penetrate beneath the conventional surface of reality and tap into a perceived vital underlying essence. The Expressionists dreamed of a radical, even violent, transformation of society. The embodiment of, and at the same time the catalyst for, that transformation was to be an extraordinary male individual, whom they called the New Man, "der neue Mensch." Writers and artists saw themselves as the prophets and even agents of that coming transformation. But these utopian hopes soon buckled under the pressure of reality: the mass slaughter in the trenches of the Western Front often gave way to visions of apocalyptic despair, and indeed there had always been only a fine line between the two.

Although Kokoschka is far better known as a painter than as a dramatist, his plays have secured him a place in theater and literary history, not least because *Murderer, Hope of Women* (1907) is acknowledged to be the first play of German Expressionism. Indeed all his plays, with the exception of *Comenius* (1936-38 / 1972), can be described as Expressionist, having been written in the period from 1907 to 1918 when Expressionism rose to become the new literary as well as artistic movement in Germany. The plays are still of importance today not only as examples of that movement but also because they shed considerable light on the artist's personal crises during this period.

Kokoschka enrolled at the Viennese School of Arts and Crafts in 1905, which provided him with a stage for his drama. *Murderer, Hope of Women* was first performed at the theater attached to this school on 4 July 1909, along with *Sphinx and Strawman*. The latter play had had its première earlier the same year at the Cabaret Fledermaus in Vienna. That Kokoschka's career as a dramatist had its roots in cabaret – there is record of an earlier shadow play called *The Speckled Egg* being performed at the same cabaret in 1907 but no text survives – is indicative of the importance he attached to mocking the conventions of the mainstream theater of his day as a way of preparing the ground for what would become the new Expressionist style of drama. Both prongs of his assault on conventional theater remained important to Kokoschka, for just as he produced four different versions of the pioneering Expressionist play *Murderer* over the next decade, so he continued to work on *Sphinx and Strawman*, producing a new version in 1913 and then transforming it into the drama *Job* (1917). And just as *Murderer* inspired the Expressionists, *Sphinx and Strawman* appealed to the anarchical Dada movement which developed out of Expressionism around 1916. It was the first play to be performed at the Dadaist Cabaret Voltaire in Zurich in 1917, an event described by Hugo Ball as the high point of Dada theater. The fact that Kokoschka continually rewrote these two plays is highly symptomatic of the experimental nature of Expressionism, as he and his contemporaries continually searched for ideological stability and a suitable artistic strategy to convey their Expressionist vision.

Sphinx and Strawman prepares the way for the creation of the new drama by breaking with the conventions of the theater prevalent at the time in a number of ways: characters address the audience directly; the figure of speech of turning someone's head is depicted literally, as is the sprouting of horns to indicate the cuckolded husband; characters are presented not as individuals but as types or even as abstract concepts (Anima as the female soul); Death twice comes on stage in dramatic fashion and then comically does nothing, saying he has lost his terror. But amidst the debunking farce – coupled with an assault on bourgeois mores – the play also shows Kokoschka grappling with an issue which is at the center of all four of his Expressionist plays, namely the conflict between Man and Woman. Indeed Avver's almost incongruously serious last speech, in which he notes that "Passion needs the spirit as a filter, otherwise it will flood body and soul, polluting both" sounds like the play's moral and owes much to the work of Otto Weininger (1880-1903), the author of the treatise *Sex and Character* which asserted the superiority of the intellectual male over the chthonic, sexual female, a thesis which exercised enormous influence over Kokoschka and many of his generation.

In *Murderer, Hope of Women*, the violence of the conflict between the sexes is indicated in the very title of the play and is reinforced not only by the action (the branding of the Woman, the stabbing of the Man), but also the violence of the language (often reduced to screams) and the stage effects, including the use of lurid colors and dramatic lighting and sound effects. Indeed, the stage directions take up as much space as the dialogue, indicating not only the extent of the stage effects but also the importance which Kokoschka attached to gesture and mime in the play. It is perhaps above all the formal experimentation in this and subsequent plays which stands as Kokoschka's greatest achievement in drama. His plays shattered the convention that theater was trying to create an illusion of reality. *Murderer*, but also *The Burning Bush* and *Job*, are characterized by extreme compression of form and language, the elimination of realistic detail, the employment of mythical, quasi biblical settings, the depiction of convulsive behavior, and a visionary, apocalyptic atmosphere. They are eloquent testimony to the sense of crisis but also of new possibilities which gripped the Expressionist imagination.

The publication of *Murderer* in Herwarth Walden's leading Expressionist journal *Der Sturm* in Berlin in 1910 caused a sensation, bringing Kokoschka's play to a wider public. The following year Kokoschka wrote a new play entitled simply *Schau-*

spiel (Play), which with small changes became *The Burning Bush*, first performed in Dresden in 1917. Here Weininger's influence on Kokoschka, and in particular the idea of the possibility of redemption through the rejection of sexuality, is most apparent. In Scene Four, the Woman describes her body as a "burning, fiery bush" and pleads with the man to put out the fire and redeem her. He rejects her desire for a physical union, whereupon she mortally wounds him by throwing a stone. But the two are reconciled in the final scene. There the Woman cradles the dying Man in her arms, grouped as in a Pietà. The message appears to be that Man can redeem both himself and Woman and bring about a transformation from superficial "seeming" to authentic "being" by rejecting physicality and focusing instead on the ascetic, spiritual dimension of life. The play is a typical heady Expressionist cocktail of quasi-religious mythology and language combined with a psychology of the sexes inspired by Weininger.

In 1912, Kokoschka met Alma Mahler, the widow of the composer Gustav Mahler, and they entered into an intense relationship which lasted until Kokoschka enlisted in the Austro-Hungarian army at the end of 1914. Traces of that relationship can be found in *The Burning Bush*, but it is in the strongly autobiographical *Orpheus and Eurydice* (1917), the most ambitious of Kokoschka's Expressionist plays, that the fullest evidence of the impact of the relationship on Kokoschka can be found. Kokoschka claimed that the play was conceived in hallucinations as he recovered from his serious war wounds in late 1915. It was at this time that he learned that Alma had aborted their child, an event which is alluded to directly in Act II, Scene 4 of the play. Kokoschka maintained that he wrote down the play from memory in 1917-1918. The play as a whole was described by Kokoschka as an attempt to rescue himself from his own chaos, as he tried to come to terms with the personal crisis he faced as a consequence not only of the ending of the relationship with Alma Mahler, but also his experience of war.

Kokoschka made free use of the Greek myth of Orpheus and Eurydice to create a bleak depiction of a doomed relationship. According to the myth, Orpheus was able to take his beloved

Eurydice from the underworld, on condition that she did not look back. Kokoschka embroidered the myth by including a second condition, namely that Orpheus may not ask Eurydice about the past. Orpheus breaks the condition and learns of Eurydice's unfaithfulness to him with Hades, the God of the Underworld. Orpheus's jealousy (often interpreted as a reference to Kokoschka's jealousy of Alma's late husband Mahler, who died in 1911 before Kokoschka met Alma) leads to the collapse of the relationship. As so often in Kokoschka's plays, the end is violent, as Eurydice strangles Orpheus, though the more peaceful epilogue does offer a measure of relief and hope after the bleakness of the main action.

Kokoschka's success as a dramatist reached its high point in the period from 1917 to 1921, when his plays were performed at major German theaters, with perhaps the highlight being the production of *The Burning Bush* at the Kammerspiele of the Deutsches Theater in Berlin in 1919 under the direction of Max Reinhardt. But after completing *Orpheus and Eurydice* in 1918, Kokoschka stopped writing plays, and after the première of that play in Frankfurt in 1921, he effectively disappeared from view as a dramatist, not least because the Expressionsit movement was by that time in sharp decline.

Throughout his life Kokoschka was fascinated by the Czech educational reformer, theologian and bishop John Amos Comenius (1592-1670). Conversations Kokoschka had about Comenius while painting the portrait of the Czech president Masaryk in 1936 (Kokoschka left Vienna in 1934 fearing an imminent takeover there by the Nazis) provided the inspiration for him to write his last play, the ambitious historical drama *Comenius*. Like Brecht in *Mother Courage and Her Children* (1938-39), Kokoschka used the setting of the Thirty Years' War (1618-48) as the backdrop for his strongly pacifist play, in which he fiercely attacked Nazism and anti-Semitism and reflected his own situation in exile. He completed a first version of the play in 1938, but it remained unpublished and unperformed at that time as Kokoschka fled to Britain in the same year, where he remained until he settled in Switzerland in 1953. The fourth act was published in 1956, but Kokoschka only took up the play again in 1972, publishing the complete play with a revised fourth act in 1973.

In the first version of Act IV, Kokoschka had made extremely explicit and pessimistic references to the situation in 1930s Germany under the Nazis. In the final version, the pessimism generated by the specific historical situation has given way to a more general pessimism and mood of resignation, with Comenius, as the mouthpiece of the dramatist, remarking, "I believe that mankind will die out, just as the giants and dinosaurs of prehistoric times did, unless we come to reason." But as so often in Kokoschka's dramas, the general pessimism is countered by a ray of hope at the end, as the little Jewish girl magically appears on the canvas of *The Night Watch*, the masterpiece of the Dutch painter Rembrandt.

Karl Leydecker

Ariadne Press
Translations

Flight from Greatness
Six Variations on Perfection
in Imperfection
By Hans Weigel
Translated by Lowell A. Bangerter

Ornament and Crime
Selected Essays
By Adolf Loos
Selected by Adolf Opel
Translated by Michael Mitchell

Ephemeral Aphorisms
By Phia Rilke
Translated by Wolfgang Mieder
and David Scrase

The Abbey
By Alois Brandstetter
Translated by Peter and
Evelyn Firchow

Stories from My Life
By Oskar Kokoschka
Translated by Michael Mitchell

The Secret of the Empire
By Heimito von Doderer
Translated by John S. Barrett

Telemachos
By Michael Köhlmeier
Translated by Edson M. Chick

The Shadow Disappears in the Sun
By Barbara Frischmuth
Translated by Nicholas J. Meyerhofer

Dona Leopoldina
The Austrian Empress of Brazil
By Gloria Kaiser
Translated by Lowell A. Bangerter

The Holy Experiment and Other Plays
By Fritz Hochwälder
Translated by Todd C. Hanlin
and Heidi Hutchinson

The Stone Breakers
and Other Novellas
By Ferdinand von Saar
Translated by Kurt and Alice Bergel

The Jib Door
By Marlen Haushofer
Translated by Jerome C. Samuelson

Quotations of a Body
By Evelyn Schlag
Translated by Willy Riemer
Prefatory Note by
Claire Tomalin

Gran Hotel Cantabria
By Heinrich von Starhemberg
Translated by Harvey I. Dunkle

Thank You, America
By Charlotte Shedd

Ariadne Press
Drama Series

*Professor Bernhardi
and Other Plays*
By Arthur Schnitzler
Translated by G.J. Weinberger

*Paracelsus
and Other One-Act Plays*
By Arthur Schnitzler
Translated by G.J. Weinberger

Three Late Plays
By Arthur Schnitzler
Translated by G.J. Weinberger

The Final Plays
By Arthur Schnitzler
Translated by G.J. Weinberger

*Seven Contemporary
Austrian Plays*
Edited by Richard H. Lawson

*Anthology of Contemporary
Austrian Folk Plays*
Translated by Richard Dixon

*New Anthology of
Austrian Folk Plays*
Edited by Richard H. Lawson

Prince and Plays
By Henry Gregor
[Heinrich von Starhemberg]
Translated by Harvey I. Dunkle

*Shooting Rats,
Other Plays and Poems*
By Peter Turrini
Translated by Richard S. Dixon

*The Slackers
and Other Plays*
By Peter Turrini
Translated by Richard S. Dixon

Dirt
By Robert Schneider
Translated by Paul F. Dvorak

*Siberia
and Other Plays*
By Felix Mitterer

*The Wild Woman
and Other Plays*
By Felix Mitterer
Translated by Todd C. Hanlin
and Heidi Hutchinson

*The Holy Experiment
and Other Plays*
By Fritz Hochwälder
Translated by Todd C. Hanlin
and Heidi Hutchinson

Five Plays
By Gerald Szyszkowitz
Translated by Todd C. Hanlin,
Heidi Hutchinson and Joseph McVeigh

Ariadne Press
Studies

*Major Figures of
Modern Austrian Literature*
Edited by Donald G. Daviau

*Major Figures of Austrian Literature
The Interwar Years 1918-1938*
Edited by Donald G. Daviau

*Major Figures of Turn-of-the-Century
Austrian Literature*
Edited by Donald G. Daviau

*Austrian Writers and the Anschluss
Understanding the Past –
Overcoming the Past*
Edited by Donald G. Daviau

*Austria in the Thirties
Culture and Politics*
Edited by Kenneth Segar
and John Warren

*Austria, 1938 - 1988
Anschluss and Fifty Years*
Edited by William E. Wright

Rilke's Duino Elegies
Edited by R.Paulin & P.Hutchinson

*Stefan Zweig
An International Bibliography*
By Randolph J. Klawiter

*Franz Karka
A Writer's Life*
By Joachim Unseld

*Kafka and Language: In the
Stream of Thoughts and Life*
By G. von Natzmer Cooper

*Of Reason and Love
The Life and Works of Marie
von Ebner-Eschenbach*
By Carl Steiner

*Marie von Ebner-Eschenbach
The Victory of a Tenacious Will*
By Doris M. Klostermaier

*"What People Call Pessimism"
Freud, Schnitzler and the 19th-Century
Controversy at the University of
Vienna Medical School*
By Mark Luprecht

*Structures of Disintegration
Narrative Strategies in Elias Canetti's
Die Blendung*
By David Darby

*Blind Reflections
Gender in Canetti's Die Blendung*
By Kristie A. Foell

*Robert Musil and the Tradition
of the German Novelle*
By Kathleen O'Connor

*Implied Dramaturgy
Robert Musil and the Crisis of Modern
Drama*
By Christian Rogowski

Ariadne Press
New Titles

The Lighted Windows
By Heimito von Doderer
Translated by John S. Barrett

*Pedro II of Brazil
Son of the Habsburg Empress*
By Gloria Kaiser
Translated by Lowell A. Bangerter

Stone's Paranoia
By Peter Henisch
Translated by Craig Decker

Footloose
By Gernot Wolfgruber
Translated by Robert Acker

International Zone
By Milo Dor and
Reinhard Federmann
Translated by Jerry Glenn and
Jennifer Kelley-Thierman

The Morning before the Journey
By Julian Schutting
Translated by Barbara Z. Schoenberg

Allemann
By Alfred Kolleritsch
Translated by Paul F. Dvorak

*Winds of Life
Destinies of a Young Viennese Jew
1938-1958*
By Gershon Evan

*Brazil
A Land of the Future*
By Stefan Zweig
Translated by Lowell A. Bangerter

The Story of Darkness
By Gerhard Roth
Translated by Helga Schreckenberger
and Jacqueline Vansant

The Traveling Years
By Elisabeth Freundlich
Translated by Elizabeth Pennebaker

*Into the Sunset
Anthology of Nineteenth-Century
Austrian Prose*
Selected and Translated by
Richard Hacken

Three Radio Plays
By Ingeborg Bachmann
Translated by Lilian Friedberg

An Anthology of Plays
By Werner Schwab
Translated by Michael Mitchell

*The Fiction of the I
Austrian Writers and Biography*
Edited by Nicholas J. Meyerhofer

*Barbara Frischmuth
in Contemporary Context*
Edited by Renate Posthofen

CPSIA information can be obtained
at www.ICGtesting.com
Printed in the USA
FSHW021039090921
84595FS